An alphabetical index to

Ulster
Emigration to
Philadelphia

1803-1850

Raymond D. Adams

CLEARFIELD

Printed for
Clearfield Company, Inc. by
Genealogical Publishing Co., Inc.
Baltimore, Maryland
1992

Reprinted for
Clearfield Company, Inc. by
Genealogical Publishing Co., Inc.
Baltimore, Maryland
1994, 1996, 1998, 2000

International Standard Book Number: 0-8063-4615-9

Made in the United States of America

Contents

iii

INTRODUCTION

Several factors contributed to the compulsory emigration from Ireland during the first half of the nineteenth century. Particularly affected was the citizenry of the province of Ulster, Protestant as well as Catholic. Ulster Scots first set the pattern of migration to America the previous century. After being lured by grants and low rents, they realized that Ireland was not the promised land after all; bad harvests, religious discrimination based on their refusal to convert to the Church of England, and high rents sent them off at the rate of 4,000 a year.

The unsuccessful rebellion of 1798, then, affected all people throughout Ireland. Although the intensity of dissatisfaction with England's grasp was confined mostly to the south and west, there was a measurable degree of support for the failed rebellion in the Ulster counties of Antrim and Down. Dissenters were mainly Protestants, some still adhering to the aims of radical Presbyterianism, but Catholics dissented as well: all diehards of the then-spent United Irishmen movement.

In the short span of three weeks 30,000 people throughout Ireland (including women and children), armed only with pitchforks and pikes, were decimated. Although the commander of government forces in Ulster granted a general amnesty to the rebels of Antrim, those of Down were shot down and left unburied in the streets. The leaders of the two main Ulster risings, McCracken and Munroe, were promptly executed. The crushing defeat of the 1798 Rebellion promoted a wide-spread fear of draconian reprisals and persecution by the Crown. This was reason enough to leave the country for freedom elsewhere.

The Act of Union between Great Britain and Ireland of January 1, 1801, was another outgrowth of the rebellion. To successfully launch the Act, British Prime Minister William Pitt was forced to bribe wealthy Protestants to give up their power and earldoms while promises of Catholic emancipation for the majority were fashioned but not really intended. The loss of a native parliament exposed an already weak home industry to competing English factories. The union with England was unfavorable to Ireland and resulted in discontentment among the poorer Protestants and a

v

sensitivity to continued oppression by the Crown among the Catholics. These were reasons enough to seek employment elsewhere.

Immigration to America continued unabated through the first half of the century, but reached its apogee in 1847 because of the devastating potato blight and resulting famine. The blight first struck without warning in 1845. Almost one half of the crop was destroyed. The people, conditioned to scarcity and want, managed to survive by salvaging what they could.

The disease struck again in June of 1846. Unlike the previous year, all of Ireland was affected by the blight before the summer's end. The potato, the main staple of the ordinary Irishman's diet, rotted in the ground with tragic results.

The disease struck again in 1847 and again in 1848. A terrible famine resulted and was rampant throughout Ireland. Before its end in 1848, the famine claimed the lives of more than a million people who died from starvation, dysentery, or the plague. Those who survived were helped financially by individuals and private charities. The British Government, rigid in attitude, did little to help. More than a million inhabitants emigrated during the famine years.

During the first half of the last century, those Irish who chose not to migrate to Canada or Australia but to America were attracted (as were their relatives and friends before them) to the larger seaport cities of New York, Boston, Philadelphia, Charleston, and New Orleans.

Each city had its own characteristics, its own advantages as well as discomforts. Philadelphia, unlike New York and Boston, presented more opportunities to the newly arrived immigrant, for it was a thriving industrial city with many foundries, leather and construction industries, textile mills, and brickyards. Jobs were accessible to the laborer and to the skilled craftsman alike.

Equally attractive to the Irish immigrant was the availability of housing at reasonable purchase prices and cheap rents. The Irish stressed the importance of owning their own homes, which many achieved after not too many years of honest work.

Perhaps another equally important reason that the city attracted the Ulster Irish was the simple fact that Philadelphia was the cradle of liberty -- living symbol of freedom from the tyranny and cruelties of British colonialism.

* * * *

This book was written to readily provide the sort of information the amateur as well as professional researcher is looking for, particularly with respect to the places of origin of the early 19th century Irish emigrant.

Research sources include a townland index first printed in Dublin in 1861, Customs Lists and Passenger Lists contained in the National Archives, existing passenger lists recorded voluntarily by ship's masters of the Cunard and Cooke shipping lines, and civil parish emigration lists retained by the Public Record Office of Northern Ireland. Extreme care has been taken in correcting the transposed spelling of townlands and place names to assure accuracy.

The principal port of departure for the early 19th century emigrants from Ulster was Londonderry, listed here as Derry. Other ports used by the shipping lines engaged in the passenger trade were Belfast, County Antrim; Newry, County Down; and Ballyshannon, County Donegal.

West Chester, Pennsylvania   Raymond D. Adams

July, 1991

ULSTER EMIGRANTS TO PHILADELPHIA

Last Name	First Name	Age	Family	Age	Address	County	Date	Ship	Port
Acheson	Sarah	--			Burnfoot	Donegal	1850	Envoy	Derry
Adair	Joanna	--	James	--	Dundrean	Donegal	1849	Superior	Derry
			William	11					
			Elizabeth	--					
Airls	William	--	Ann	--	Lowtherstown	Fermanagh	1847	Montpellier	Derry
			Robert	6m					
Alcorn	Andrew	20	Martha	20	Ballynary	Derry	1833-34	--	Derry
Alcorn	Ann	--	Robert	--	Waterside	Derry	1850	Superior	Derry
Alcorn	Francis	--	& Wife	--	--	--	1811	Fame	Derry
Alcorn	James	--			--	--	1811	Fame	Derry
Alcorn	John	--	& Family	--	--	--	1811	Fame	Derry
Alcorn	Joseph	--			--	--	1811	Fame	Derry
Alexander	Isabella	--			Maghera	Donegal	1847	Venice	Derry
Alexander	Jane	--			Omagh	Tyrone	1847	Hartford	Derry
Alexander	William	32	Jane	30	Donaghadee	Down	1803	Mohawk	Derry
			James	11					
			Martha	10					
Allan	Unfty	--			Castlefin	Donegal	1847	Allegheny	Derry
Allen	Andrew	--			Convoy	Donegal	1850	Lumley	Derry
Allen	George	26			Ballyriskmore	Derry	1833-34	--	Derry
Alley	Stephen	24			L'Derry	Derry	1803	Brutus	Derry
Allis	Tera	30	James	14	Drimahy	Donegal	1804	Catherine	Ballyshannon
Anderson	Archd.	19			Armagh	Armagh	1803	Mohawk	Derry
Anderson	Henry	46			--	--	1804	Maria	Derry
Anderson	Hugh	--	Ann	--	--	--	1811	Harmony	Derry
			James	--					
Anderson	James	--			--	--	1811	Fame	Derry
Anderson	James	--			St.Johnstown	Donegal	1847	Allegheny	Derry
Anderson	John	28			--	--	1804	Maria	Derry
Anderson	Margaret	--	Robert	--	Coagh	Tyrone	1849	Superior	Derry
			MaryAnn	--					
			George	--					
			Rachel	--					

1

ULSTER EMIGRANTS TO PHILADELPHIA

Last Name	First Name	Age	Family	Age	Address	County	Date	Ship	Port
			Jane	11					
			John	10					
Anderson	Margaret	36			--	--	1804	Maria	Derry
Anderson	Mary	24	Mary	2	--	Down	1803	Strafford	Derry
Anderson	Samuel	46			--	--	1804	Maria	Derry
Anderson	William	53			--	--	1804	Maria	Derry
Andrews	Gabriel	--			--	--	1811	Mary	Derry
Armstrong	Alexander	29			--	Armagh	1803	Patty	Newry
Armstrong	Edward	--			Lowtherstown	Fermanagh	1847	Montpellier	Derry
Armstrong	Jane	--			Omagh	Tyrone	1849	Envoy	Derry
Armstrong	John	29			--	Down	1803	Patty	Newry
Armstrong	Margaret	--			Kesh	Fermanagh	1850	Superior	Derry
Armstrong	Mathew	23			Ballindrait	Donegal	1803	Penna.	Derry
Armstrong	Samuel	--			Omagh	Tyrone	1847	Montpellier	Derry
Armstrong	Thomas	31	Mary	27	Clonfeacle	Armagh	1803	George	Belfast
Arskine	Joseph	56			--	--	1804	Maria	Derry
Arthur	James	--			--	--	1811	Fame	Derry
Arthur	John	--			Coleraine	Derry	1849	Garland	Derry
Arthur	Nancy	--			Ballybofey	Donegal	1848	Hannah Kerr	Derry
Ash	David	--			Ballykelly	Derry	1848	MaryCampbell	Derry
Askin	Elizabeth	--			Muff	Derry	1849	Garland	Derry
Aston	Sarah	--			L'Derry	Derry	1849	Superior	Derry
Atwell	Robert	--			Omagh	Tyrone	1847	Hartford	Derry
Aull	James	--			Magilligan	Derry	1849	Garland	Derry
Awl	Margaret	--	Martha	--	Limavady	Derry	1847	Hartford	Derry
Bacon	William	28	Elizabeth	27	Taughblane	Down	1803	Mohawk	Derry
			William	12					
Bailey	Esther	--			--	--	1811	Fame	Derry
Bailey	George	--	Sarah	--	Lifford	(*)	1850	Envoy	Derry
			George	7					
			David	5					
			Stewart	3					
			Matty Jane	9m					

(*) See Endnotes

Last Name	First Name	Age	Family	Age	Address	County	Date	Ship	Port
Bailey	Thomas	--			Omagh	Tyrone	1850	Envoy	Derry
Bailie	Mathew	48	Elizabeth	46	Clough	Down	1804	Commerce	--
			Stewart	20					
			Matty	18					
Bain	Patrick	--			Buncrana	Donegal	1850	Superior	Derry
Baird	David	--			Hornhead?	?	1847	Barbara	Derry
Baird	James	58	William	28	Ballymore	Derry	1833-34	--	Derry
			James, Jr.	23					
			John	9					
			Ann	30					
			Elenor	17					
			Mary Ann	14					
			Martha	7					
Ballantine	William	--			N'tnstewart	Tyrone	1847	Superior	Derry
Bannin	Michael	--			L'Derry	Derry	1849	Superior	Derry
Barber	Rebecca	10	John	8	Limavady	Derry	1849	Envoy	Derry
			Thomas	6					
			James	4					
Barlow	William	--			Enniskillen	Fermanagh	1850	Envoy	Derry
Barnett	Andrew	24	Annabella	20	--	--	1803	Active	Newry
Barnett	Elizabeth	16	Jane	12	--	--	1803	Active	Newry
Barnett	John	38	Margaret	34	--	--	1803	Active	Newry
Barr	Margaret	--	MarthaJane	--	Muff	Derry	1849	Garland	Derry
			Sarah	--					
Bates	John	21			Dunnamanagh	Derry	1803	Mohawk	Derry
Baun	Ann	--			Stranorlar	Donegal	1847	Allegheny	Derry
Baxter	WIlliam	--			Omagh	Tyrone	1849	Superior	Derry
Bayle	Darby	24	Jean	21	Letterkenny	Donegal	1803	Brutus	Derry
Beattie	William	--	Rebecca	--	N'tnstewart	Tyrone	1848	MaryCampbell	Derry
Beatty	Catherine	--			Lowtherstown	Fermanagh	1850	Envoy	Derry
Beatty	Jane	--			Dunfanaghy	Derry	1847	Hershell	Derry
Beatty	Patrick	--			Moville	Donegal	1849	Envoy	Derry
Beatty	Thomas	--	Margaret	--	Fahan	Donegal	1848	HannahKerr	Derry
Beatty	William	--	Jane	--	--	--	1811	Mary	Derry

3

ULSTER EMIGRANTS TO PHILADELPHIA

Last Name	First Name	Age	Family	Age	Address	County	Date	Ship	Port
			George	--					
Beck	James	30	John	25	Ardaghy	Down	1804	Commerce	--
			Mararet	24					
Beers	Hugh	--			Ballymoney	Antrim	1849	Garland	Derry
Bellman	John	35			--	--	1804	Maria	Derry
Bellman	Samuel	33			--	--	1804	Maria	Derry
Bennett	Z.	--			--	--	1811	Mary	Derry
Benson	Elizabeth	--			Whitecastle	Donegal	1847	MaryStewart	Derry
Benson	Richard	--			Kilmacrenan	Donegal	1850	Envoy	Derry
Bingham	William	14			--	--	1803	Edward	Belfast
Black	Andrew	--			Limavady	Derry	1847	Hershell	Derry
Black	Stewart	--			Convoy	Donegal	1849	Superior	Derry
Blackburne	Letitia	--			Omagh	Tyrone	1850	Envoy	Derry
Blair	Andrew	--			Coleraine	Derry	1849	Garland	Derry
Blair	George	--	Jane	--	--	--	1811	Harmony	Derry
			Catherine	--					
			William	--					
Blair	James	--			--	--	1811	Harmony	Derry
Blair	James	--	Elizabeth	--	--	--	1811	Harmony	Derry
Blair	James	22			Ballywildrick	Derry	1834	--	Derry
Blair	John	29			--	Down	1803	Patty	Newry
Blair, Sr.	James	26	Mary	20	Ballywildrick	Derry	1833	--	Derry
Blaney	Patrick	--	Susan	--	Millford	Donegal	1848	HannahKerr	Derry
Blany	Fanny	--	Henry	--	Omagh	Tyrone	1847	Venice	Derry
			John	11					
			Robert	7					
			Jane	5					
Bleakley	John	--			Upr. Drumons	Derry	1833-34	--	Derry
Bloomer	Thomas	--	Elizabeth	--	Cookstown	Tyrone	1847	Hartford	Derry
Blumes?	Ann	--			Aughnacloy	(*)	1850	Superior	Derry
Bogan	Paul	--			Caven	Donegal	1847	Barbara	Derry
Boles	Bennet	23			Stewartstown	Tyrone	1803	Brutus	Derry
Bonar	James	--			Ramelton	Donegal	1850	Envoy	Derry

(*) See Endnotes

4

ULSTER EMIGRANTS TO PHILADELPHIA

Last Name	First Name	Age	Family	Age	Address	County	Date	Ship	Port
Bond	John	32	Anne	27	Bratwell	Derry	1834	--	Derry
			Mary	5					
			Margaret	2					
			Barbara	2					
Boner	Harriett	--			Stranorlar	Donegal	1849	Envoy	Derry
Boner	Robert	--	Ann Jane	--	Ramelton	Donegal	1847	Hartford	Derry
			Catherine	--					
Borland	Alex	--			Rosnakill	Donegal	1850	Envoy	Derry
Boulston	John	--			St.Johnstown	Donegal	1847	Allegheny	Derry
Boyce	James	40	Ann	38	Lisnamuck	Derry	1833-34	--	Derry
			John	18					
			James	16					
			David	13					
			Leslie	10					
Boyd	Henry	40			Tullans	Derry	1833-34	--	Derry
Boyd	James	26			Pettigoe	(*)	1804	Brothers	Derry
Boyd	James	26			St.Johnston	Donegal	1803	Penna.	Derry
Boyd	Matilda	--			Waterside	Derry	1847	Venice	Derry
Boyd	Robert	--	Sarah	--	N'tnstewart	Tyrone	1847	Hershell	Derry
			Letitia	--					
			AnnEliza	11					
			Isabella	11					
Boyd	Samuel	--	Ellen	--	--		--	1811	Harmony	Derry
			MaryAnn	--					
Boyle	Ann	--	Biddy	--	Dunfanaghy	Donegal	1848	MaryCampbell	Derry
Boyle	Biddy	--			Dunfanaghy	Donegal	1848	MaryCampbell	Derry
Boyle	Bridget	--	Magy	5	Rosses	Sligo	1847	Hartford	Derry
			Ann	3					
			Nora	3					
			Michael	2					
			Bridget	1m					
			Peggy	--					
Boyle	Catherine	--			Dunfanaghy	Donegal	1850	Lumley	Derry

(*) See Endnotes

5

ULSTER EMIGRANTS TO PHILADELPHIA

Last Name	First Name	Age	Family	Age	Address	County	Date	Ship	Port
Boyle	Daniel	--			Dunfanaghy	Donegal	1848	MaryCampbell	Derry
Boyle	James	--			Convoy	Donegal	1847	Hartford	Derry
Boyle	James	40			Ballyshannon	Donegal	1804	Brothers	Derry
Boyle	John	--			L'Derry	Derry	1847	Allegheny	Derry
Boyle	John	--	Daniel	--	Rosses	Sligo	1847	Hartford	Derry
			Charles	--					
			John	13					
			Bridget	--					
			Mary	--					
Boyle	Manus	--	Mary	--	Convoy	Donegal	1849	Superior	Derry
			Mary	6					
Boyle	Patrick	--	Mrs.	--	Dunfanaghy	Donegal	1848	MaryCampbell	Derry
			Catherine	--					
			Margaret	--					
			Biddy	--					
			John	--					
			James	--					
			William	2					
Boyle	Rose	--			Gidore	?	1847	Hartford	Derry
Boyle	William	--			Letterkenny	Donegal	1849	Superior	Derry
Bradley	Biddy	--			Gortin	(*)	1847	Montpellier	Derry
Bradley	Eleanor	--			Castlegrove	Galway	1850	Superior	Derry
Bradley	Mary	--			Beragh	Tyrone	1847	Venice	Derry
Bradley	Mary	--			Culdaff	Donegal	1848	HannahKerr	Derry
Bradley	Oliver	--			Draperstown	Derry	1850	Superior	Derry
Bradley	Patrick	--			Draperstown	Derry	1849	Garland	Derry
Bradley	Sally	--			Draperstown	Derry	1850	Superior	Derry
Bradley	William	--	Patrick	--	Gortin	(*)	1847	MaryStewart	Derry
Brannen	Catherine	--			Magilligan	Derry	1847	Allegheny	Derry
Brannon	James	--			Dunkineely	Tyrone	1850	Superior	Derry
Brattan	Martha	--			Donaghadee	Down	1847	Venice	Derry
Bratten	George	--			Londonderry	Derry	1847	Hershell	Derry
Breen	Terrence	--	Patrick	--	Letterkenny	Donegal	1847	Venice	Derry

(*) See Endnotes

ULSTER EMIGRANTS TO PHILADELPHIA

Last Name	First Name	Age	Family	Age	Address	County	Date	Ship	Port
			Alice	--					
			Catherine	--					
			Rosanna	--					
Breeson	Hugh	40			Tullaghan	Donegal	1803	Penna.	Derry
‿Breson	Bridget	--	Michael	--	Claudy	Derry	1850	Superior	Derry
			John	11					
Brian	Hugh	28			Tullans	Derry	1833-34	--	Derry
Brigham	David	22			Ballyshannon	Donegal	1803	Penna.	Derry
Brigham	Elizabeth	26			Ballyshannon	Donegal	1803	Penna.	Derry
Brigham	Ezekial	25			Ballyshannon	Donegal	1803	Penna.	Derry
Brigham	Jane	25			Ballyshannon	Donegal	1803	Penna.	Derry
Brigham	John	20			Dungiven	Derry	1803	Penna.	Derry
Brison	Susan	--	Catherine	8	Carndonagh	Donegal	1847	Superior	Derry
			William	2					
Brodley	Alexander	28			N'tnstewart	Tyrone	1803	Mohawk	Derry
Brodley	Patrick	19			L'Derry	Derry	1803	Mohawk	Derry
Brogan	Dennis	--			Dunfanaghy	Donegal	1848	MaryCampbell	Derry
Brogan	James	--			Crossroads	Donegal	1850	Envoy	Derry
Brogan	John	--			Kilmacrenan	Donegal	1849	Garland	Derry
Broson	John	--	Mary Ann	--	Strabane	Tyrone	1850	Envoy	Derry
Brosters	Thomas	20	Mary	18	Glebe	Derry	1833	--	Derry
			Jane	20					
Brouster	James	--	Samuel	13	Coleraine	Derry	1847	Venice	Derry
			James	11					
Brown	Ann	--			--	--	1811	Mary	Derry
Brown	Biddy	38			--	Down	1803	Patty	Newry
Brown	Eliza	--			Castlederg	Tyrone	1848	MaryCampbell	Derry
Brown	Ellen	--			Donegal	Donegal	1850	Lumley	Derry
Brown	Francis	--			Strabane	Tyrone	1850	Superior	Derry
Brown	Margaret	--			Ballindrait	Donegal	1847	MaryStewart	Derry
Brown	Mary	--			Newbuildings	(*)	1849	Garland	Derry
Brown	Mary	--			Strabane	Tyrone	1850	Envoy	Derry
Brown	Matthew	18			Drumhome	Donegal	1804	Catherine	Bally-(*) shannon

(*) See Endnotes

7

Last Name	First Name	Age	Family	Age	Address	County	Date	Ship	Port
Brown	Patrick	--			Millford	Donegal	1848	MaryCampbell	Derry
Brown	Patrick	--			Raphoe	Donegal	1849	Envoy	Derry
Brown	William	--			Lowtherstown	Fermanagh	1847	Montpellier	Derry
Brown	William	--	Margaret	--	Letterkenny	Donegal	1850	Lumley	Derry
			James	--					
			Samuel	--					
Brown	William	30			Limavady	Derry	1833-34	--	Derry
Browne	Catherine	--			Letterkenny	Donegal	1850	Envoy	Derry
Browne	Mary	--			--	--	1811	Harmony	Derry
Browne	Patrick	--	Bridget	--	--	--	1811	Harmony	Derry
Bruce	William	--			Ramelton	Dongal	1847	Venice	Derry
Bruston	Sarah	--			Coleraine	Derry	1850	Envoy	Derry
Buchannon	Rebecca	--			Millford	Donegal	1847	Allegheny	Derry
Buchanon	Alexander	9	Edward	7	Ballybofey	Donegal	1848	HannahKerr	Derry
			William	3					
Buchanon	James A.	--			St.Johnstown	Donegal	1847	Hartford	Derry
Buchanon	Jane	--	MaryJane	12	Ballybofey	Donegal	1848	HannahKerr	Derry
Buchanon	Uriah	--	Mary	--	Millford	Donegal	1848	MaryCampbell	Derry
			Martha	--					
Buchanon	Watt	--	Jane	--	Ramelton	Donegal	1847	Hershell	Derry
			Eliza	--					
			Margery	--					
			James	12					
			Watt	9					
			Jane	6					
			David	4					
Bull	Mary	--			--	--	1811	Harmony	Derry
Bullion	Biddy	--			Limavady	Derry	1850	Envoy	Derry
Burgery	Peter	--			Clanely	Tyrone	1850	Envoy	Derry
Burke	Catherine	--			Ballybofey	Donegal	1848	HannahKerr	Derry
Burke	Ellen	--			Gortin	(*)	1849	Envoy	Derry
Burke	Francis	--			Gallagh	(*)	1850	Superior	Derry
Burke	Francis	40	Mary	30	Cornamuckla	Derry	1833-34	--	Derry

(*) See Endnotes

ULSTER EMIGRANTS TO PHILADELPHIA

Last Name	First Name	Age	Family	Age	Address	County	Date	Ship	Port
Burke	John	--	Rosey	--	Learmount	Derry	1847	Hershell	Derry
			Thomas	6					
			John	4					
			James	2					
			Charles	3m					
Burke	Thomas	--			Letterkenny	Donegal	1848	MaryCampbell	Derry
Burns	Daniel	--			Coleraine	Derry	1849	Superior	Derry
Burns	James	20			--	--	1803	Edward	Belfast
Burns	Rose	--			Gortin	(*)	1850	Superior	Derry
Busby, Jr.	Robert	24			Ballymore	Derry	1833-34	--	Derry
Byst	Nathaniel	30			Ganaby	Antrim	1803	George	Belfast
Cairns	William	--			Beragh	Tyrone	1849	Superior	Derry
Caldwell	Mary	--			Omagh	Tyrone	1847	Hartford	Derry
Callaghan	Ann	--			Carrigan	Donegal	1847	Hartford	Derry
Callaghan	Catherine	--			Malin	Donegal	1849	Garland	Derry
Callaghan	Eliza Jane	--			Donaghadee	Down	1850	Envoy	Derry
Callaghan	Kerty	--			Malin	Donegal	1850	Envoy	Derry
Callaghan	Mary	--			Rosnakill	Donegal	1847	MaryStewart	Derry
Callaghan	Nancy	--			Dunnamanagh	Derry	1849	Garland	Derry
Callaghan	Nancy	--			L'Derry	Derry	1849	Superior	Derry
Callaghan	Neal	19			Ardmalin	Donegal	1803	Mohawk	Derry
Callaghan	Nelly	--			Malin	Donegal	1848	MaryCampbell	Derry
Callaughan	Thomas	23			Strabane	Tyrone	1803	Brutus	Derry
Callen	James	--			Coagh	Tyrone	1849	Superior	Derry
Callen	John	--			Castlegrove	Galway	1850	Lumley	Derry
Callighan	Pat	--			Carne	Donegal	1847	Hartford	Derry
Campbell	Andrew	--			Ture	Donegal	1850	Envoy	Derry
Campbell	Ann	--	Rebecca	--	Dunnamanagh	Derry	1847	Superior	Derry
			JaneAnn	12					
			David	3					
Campbell	Anthony	--			--	--	1811	Mary	Derry
Campbell	Bernard	--	Catherine	--	Glenties	Donegal	1847	Barbara	Derry
			John	--					

(*) See Endnotes

Last Name	First Name	Age	Family	Age	Address	County	Date	Ship	Port
			Biddy	--					
			Bernard	10					
			Daniel	7					
			Cicily	5					
Campbell	James	--			Omagh	Tyrone	1847	Montpellier	Derry
Campbell	James	--	Nancy	--	Ture	Donegal	1847	Superior	Derry
Campbell	James	28	Mary	20	Dungannon	Tyrone	1803	Mohawk	Derry
Campbell	John	--	Fanny	--	Ballykelly	Derry	1847	Hartford	Derry
Campbell	Nancy	--			L'Derry	Derry	1848	HannahKerr	Derry
Campbell	Nancy	--	Margaret	--	Draperstown	Derry	1849	Garland	Derry
			Mary	--					
Campbell	Thomas	--			Beragh	Tyrone	1849	Garland	Derry
Campbell	William	--	Ann (W)	--	Plumbridge	Derry	1847	Superior	Derry
			James	11					
			Matilda	7					
			Jane	1					
Candea	John	--	Catherine	--	Omagh	Tyrone	1847	Venice	Derry
			James	13					
			Margaret	11					
			Ann Jane	9					
			John	7					
			Matilda	4					
			Elizabeth	1					
Canney	Charles	28			Tullaghan	Donegal	1803	Penna.	Derry
Canning	Daniel	--			L'Derry	Derry	1850	Envoy	Derry
Canning	David	24			Collins	Derry	1833-34	--	Derry
Canning	John	18	Marcus	18	Largyreagh	Derry	1833-34	--	Derry
			Annyan	11					
Cannivan	Maria	--	Letitia	--	Limavady	Derry	1847	MaryStewart	Derry
Cannon	Margaret	--			--	--	1847	Superior	Derry
Cannon	William	--			Clougheneely	Donegal	1847	Venice	Derry
Carey	William	--	Ann	--	Carndonaghy	Antrim	1847	Hartford	Derry
			William	--					
			Jane	7					

ULSTER EMIGRANTS TO PHILADELPHIA

Last Name	First Name	Age	Family	Age	Address	County	Date	Ship	Port
Carey	William	--	Ann	--	Templemoyle	(*)	1847	Allegheny	Derry
			Mary	--					
			Jane	--					
Carlain	Michael	26			Killybegs	Donegal	1804	Catherine	Bally-shannon
Carlin	ELizabeth	--			Moville	Donegal	1847	Hartford	Derry
Carlin	Hannah	--			Clougheneely	Donegal	1848	MaryCampbell	Derry
Carlin	John	--	Sarah	--	Strabane	Tyrone	1847	MaryStewart	Derry
			Michael	13					
			Catherine	11					
			William	9					
			Hugh	7					
			Jane	5					
			John	1					
Carlin	Margaret	--			Gortin	(*)	1847	Montpellier	Derry
Carlin	Mary	--	Patrick	--	Kilmacrenan	Donegal	1847	MaryStewart	Derry
			James	--					
Carlin	Michael	--			Moville	Donegal	1850	Envoy	Derry
Carlin	William	--			Moville	Donegal	1850	Superior	Derry
Carlind	Isabella	--			N'tncunningham	Donegal	1849	Garland	Derry
Carolan	Rose	--			--	--	1811	Fame	Derry
Carr	James	--			Rosnakill	Donegal	1849	Superior	Derry
Carr	William	20			--	--	1803	Strafford	Derry
Carrolton	Catherine	--			Ederny	Fermanagh	1849	Garland	Derry
Cartin	Michael	28	Mary Ann	28	Tarnakelly	Derry	1833-34	--	Derry
Cartin	Nancy	--	Mary	--	Learmount	Derry	1847	Hershell	Derry
Cartly	Mary	--	Alexander	--	Omagh	Tyrone	1850	Superior	Derry
			Samuel	10					
			Margaret	8					
			Catherine	6					
			Mary	--					
Carton	John	35			Clagan	Derry	1803	Mohawk	Derry
Caskey	Martha Jane	--			Limavady	Derry	1850	Envoy	Derry

(*) See Endnotes

Last Name	First Name	Age	Family	Age	Address	County	Date	Ship	Port
Caskey	Samuel	50	Ann	47	Drumore	Derry	1833-34	--	Derry
			John	22					
			Mary	24					
			Eliz.	22					
			Ann	20					
			Milly	18					
Cassidy	Ann	--	Mary	--	Maghera	Donegal	1849	Envoy	Derry
			Roddy	--					
Cassidy	Hugh	--	Sarah	--	Coleraine	Derry	1850	Envoy	Derry
Cassidy	Jane	--			Cross Roads	Donegal	1847	Hershell	Derry
Cavanagh	Edward	--			Claudy	Derry	1847	Hershell	Derry
Ceahy	James	20			Ardmore	Derry	1833-34	--	Derry
Ceyrin	William	--			--	--	1811	Mary	Derry
Chamber	John	20			--	Tyrone	1803	Strafford	Derry
Chambers	Andrew	--	Margaret	--	Millford	Donegal	1848	MaryCampbell	Derry
Chambers	John	--			Grorty?	?	1847	Barbara	Derry
Chambers	John	--			Redcastle	Queens	1849	Garland	Derry
Chambers	John	--			Strabane	Tyrone	1847	Allegheny	Derry
Chambers	Mary Ann	--			N'tnstewart	Tyrone	1847	Montpellier	Derry
Chambers	Robert	--	Margaret	--	Glenalla	Donegal	1847	Allegheny	Derry
Chambers	William	--			Glenfin	Roscommon	1850	Superior	Derry
Chestnut	Isabella	--	Samuel	--	Kilmacrenan	Donegal	1847	MaryStewart	Derry
			Margaret	--					
			Benjamin	--					
			George	11					
Chestnut	Samuel	--			--	--	1811	Harmony	Derry
Chisen	George	--	Eliza	--	Castlederg	Tyrone	1848	MaryCampbell	Derry
Clark	David	--			--	--	1811	Mary	Derry
Clark	William	--	Ann	--	--	--	1811	Mary	Derry
Clarke	Edward	--			Fahan	Donegal	1847	Hartford	Derry
Clarke	Edward	40			Enniskillen	Fermanagh	1803	Strafford	Derry
Clarke	James	--			Stranorlar	Donegal	1847	Allegheny	Derry
Clarke	Jane	--			Ramelton	Donegal	1849	Superior	Derry
Clarke	John	20			Ballywildrick	Derry	1833	--	Derry

ULSTER EMIGRANTS TO PHILADELPHIA

Last Name	First Name	Age	Family	Age	Address	County	Date	Ship	Port
Clarke	Mary	--			Ballybofey	Donegal	1848	HannahKerr	Derry
Clarke	Mary	--			St.Johnstown	Donegal	1849	Garland	Derry
Clarke	Mary J.	--			Trimragh	Donegal	1847	Hartford	Derry
Clarke	Samuel	--	Jane	--	Claudy	Derry	1847	Barbara	Derry
			Matilda	--					
			Eliza	--					
Clary	John	--			--	--	1811	Mary	Derry
Clendining	James	18			N'tnconningham	Donegal	1803	Brutus	Derry
Clide	Elizabeth	--			Omagh	Tyrone	1847	Venice	Derry
Clyne	John	21			Terrydoo	Derry	1833-34	--	Derry
Cochran	Ann	--	Hugh	--	Coleraine	Derry	1849	Superior	Derry
Cochran	Isaac	27			Ballynacally	Derry	1803	Brutus	Derry
Cochran	James	--			Cumber	Derry	1847	Montpellier	Derry
Cochran	James	--	Matilda	--	Ballykelly	Derry	1847	Hartford	Derry
			William	11					
			Matilda	9					
			Isabella	8					
			Robert	7					
			Adessa	6					
			Mary	4					
			Elizabeth	2					
Cochran	John	--			--	--	1811	Harmony	Derry
Cochran	John	--			Coleraine	Derry	1847	Hartford	Derry
Cochrane	Andrew	24			Ballinlees	Derry	1833-34	--	Derry
Coleman	Ann	--			Limavady	Derry	1850	Envoy	Derry
Colhoun	Andrew	--			Omagh	Tyrone	1847	Barbara	Derry
Coll	Betty	--	Biddy	--	Claudy	Derry	1849	Garland	Derry
Coll	Charles	--			Rathmullan	Donegal	1847	Montpellier	Derry
Coll	Dennis	--			Dunfanaghy	Donegal	1848	MaryCampbell	Derry
Coll	Mary	--			Fanad	Donegal	1847	Hershell	Derry
Coll	Owen	--			Beragh	Tyrone	1849	Superior	Derry
Collins	Catherine	--			L'Derry	Derry	1850	Superior	Derry
Collins	John	--			Cappagh	Donegal	1847	Hartford	Derry
Colvin	Jane	--			--	--	1811	Harmony	Derry

ULSTER EMIGRANTS TO PHILADELPHIA

Last Name	First Name	Age	Family	Age	Address	County	Date	Ship	Port
Colvin	John	--			--	--	1811	Harmony	Derry
Conaghan	Isabella	--			Carrigan	Donegal	1847	Allegheny	Derry
Conaghan	Mary	--	Margaret	8	L'Derry	Derry	1847	Venice	Derry
			James	6					
Conigan	Elizabeth	--			Lowtherstown	Fermanagh	1847	Montpellier	Derry
Conigan	Henry	--	Jane	--	Lowtherstown	Fermanagh	1847	Montpellier	Derry
			Isabella	11					
			Jane	9m					
Conigham	Thomas	18			Ballymoney	Antrim	1803	Strafford	Derry
Connel	Jane	--			Coleraine	Derry	1847	Superior	Derry
Connelly	Patrick	--			--	--	1811	Mary	Derry
Connelly	Patrick	33			Rossinver	Leitrim	1804	Jefferson	Bally-shannon
Connelly	Rose	31			Rossinver	Leitrim	1804	Jefferson	Bally-shannon
Conner	Bridget	--			Lowtherstown	Fermanagh	1849	Garland	Derry
Conner	James	--			Omagh	Tyrone	1847	Montpellier	Derry
Conner	Pat	12			Dungiven	Derry	1849	Garland	Derry
Connolly	William	--			Ballyshannon	Donegal	1849	Envoy	Derry
Connor	Cecil	--	Patrick	8	Maghera	Donegal	1850	Superior	Derry
			John	6					
Connor	John	--			Drumcliffe	Sligo	1804	Jefferson	Ballys-hannon
Conoly	Owen	--	Ann	--	L'Derry	Derry	1848	HannahKerr	Derry
			Charles	--					
			Susanna	--					
Conway	Charles	--	Martha	--	Claudy	Derry	1849	Garland	Derry
			James	13					
			Margaret	13					
			• Bridget	11					
			Nancy	9					
			Mary	7					
			Rosey	5					
			Martha	3					

Last Name	First Name	Age	Family	Age	Address	County	Date	Ship	Port
Conway	James	--			Castlegrove	Galway	1850	Lumley	Derry
Conway	Mary Ann	--			Ramelton	Donegal	1847	Superior	Derry
Conway	Michael	--	Dennis	--	Strabane	Tyrone	1847	Allegheny	Derry
			Ann	--					
Conway	Neill	9m			Claudy	Derry	1849	Garland	Derry
Conway	Peter	--			Gortin	(*)	1847	Montpellier	Derry
Conway	Peter	--	Hannah	--	Ramelton	Donegal	1847	Hartford	Derry
			Bernard	13					
			Rose	7					
Conway	Rose	--			Gortin	(*)	1847	Hartford	Derry
Conyngham	Andrew	34	Elitia	34	Lochris	Donegal	1804	Catherine	Bally-shannon
			John	12					
			Andrew	6					
Conyngham	George	49	Alexander	21	Monargan	Donegal	1804	Catherine	Bally-shannon
			James	18					
			John	15					
			Catherine	12					
Conyngham	John	55	Isabella	49	Monargan	Donegal	1804	Catherine	Bally-shannon
Conyngham	William	26	Isabella	23	Monargan	Donegal	1804	Catherine	Ballys-shannon
Cooke	Martha	--			L'Derry	Derry	1850	Superior	Derry
Cooke	Thomas	--			L'Derry	Derry	1850	Superior	Derry
Cooney	Bridget	--			Ballyshannon	Donegal	1849	Superior	Derry
Cooney	Bryan	--			--	--	1811	Harmony	Derry
Coragan	Ellen	--			Kesh	Fermanagh	1850	Envoy	Derry
Corner	Rebecca	--			Limavady	Derry	1850	Envoy	Derry
Corrin	Farrigle	--			Creeslough	Donegal	1847	MaryStewart	Derry
Corsaden	James	--			Ballybofey	Donegal	1848	HannahKerr	Derry
Corscaden	Catherine	--	Margaret	--	Donegal	Donegal	1847	Barbara	Derry
Corscadin	Arthur	--			Letterkenny	Donegal	1847	Venice	Derry

(*) See Endnotes

ULSTER EMIGRANTS TO PHILADELPHIA

Last Name	First Name	Age	Family	Age	Address	County	Date	Ship	Port
Coulter	John	--			Pettigoe	(*)	1850	Superior	Derry
Courtney	Richard	25	Margaret	24	Clough	Down	1804	Commerce	--
Cowan	Mary	--			Ballybofey	Donegal	1848	HannahKerr	Derry
Coway	John	--			N'tnstewart	Tyrone	1849	Garland	Derry
Coyle	Anne	--			Letterkenny	Donegal	1850	Lumley	Derry
Coyle	Hanna	--			Millford	Donegal	1847	Superior	Derry
Coyle	John	--	Daniel	--	--	--	1811	Harmony	Derry
Coyle	Thomas	--			Crossroads	Donegal	1847	Montpellier	Derry
Craig	John	20			Sistrakeel	Derry	1833-34	--	Derry
Craig	Martha	--			Dungiven	Derry	1847	Allegheny	Derry
Craig	Mary	--			Claudy	Derry	1847	Superior	Derry
Craig	Roseann	--			Elagh	Tyrone	1849	Garland	Derry
Craig	Ross	--	Ellizabeth	--	Limavady	Derry	1849	Envoy	Derry
			Sarah	--					
Craig	Thomas	--	William	--	Dungiven	Derry	1847	Allegheny	Derry
Craig	William	--			--	--	1811	Mary	Derry
Craven	Jno.	25			--	--	1803	Edward	Belfast
Crawford	Charles	--	Rosanna	--	SixMileCross	Tyrone	1849	Envoy	Derry
			MaryAnn	--					
			John	12					
			Margaret	9					
			ElizaJane	7					
			Arthur	4					
			Charles	2					
			Matilda	6m					
			Rebecca	6m					
Crawford	Joseph	26			Culmore	Derry	1833-34	--	Derry
Crawford	Martha	--			Moboy	(*)	1847	Venice	Derry
Crawford	Martin	--	Eliz.	--	Downhill	Derry	1847	Hartford	Derry
			Peggy	--					
			PeggyJane	8					
			Nancy	4					
			Robert	2					

(*) See Endnotes

Last Name	First Name	Age	Family	Age	Address	County	Date	Ship	Port
Crawford	MaryAnn	--			Monksfield	Galway	1847	Barbara	Derry
Crawford	Sarah	--			Portrush	Antrim	1850	Lumley	Derry
Creighton	Hugh	--			Ballybofey	Donegal	1848	HannahKerr	Derry
Creiton	Ann	22	Fanny	24	Lisnamuck	Derry	1833-34	--	Derry
Creswell	James	--	Elizabeth	--	Moville	Donegal	1847	Hartford	Derry
			Mary	8					
			Samuel	6					
			John	4					
			Elizabeth	1					
Crocket	George	--	Samuel	--	--	--	1811	Fame	Derry
Crockett	George	--	John	--	--	--	1811	Fame	Derry
			Robert	--					
Cross	Elizabeth	--			--	--	1811	Fame	Derry
Crossan	Charles	--	Charles	--	L'Derry	Derry	1850	Envoy	Derry
Crossen	Cornelius	--			--	--	1811	Mary	Derry
Crosson	Patrick	--			--	--	1811	Mary	Derry
Crothers	John	--	Ann	--	Moville	Donegal	1847	Montpellier	Derry
			James	--					
			MaryAnn	11					
			Robert	9					
			John	6					
Crumlisk	Mary	--			Dunkineely	Tyrone	1850	Superior	Derry
Cruse	James	--	Henry	--	Ballykelly	Derry	1848	MaryCampbell	Derry
Cue	Patrick	22			Aughnacloy	(*)	1803	Brutus	Derry
Culbert	George	--			--	--	1811	Fame	Derry
Cullen	Francis	16			Rossinver	Leitrim	1804	Jefferson	Bally-shannon
Cullen	James	--			--	--	1811	Harmony	Derry
Cummings	John	--			--	--	1811	Mary	Derry
Cunningham	Jane	12	Robert	10	Ballybofey	Donegal	1848	HannahKerr	Derry
Cunningham	John	--	Mary	--	Dungiven	Derry	1848	HannahKerr	Derry
			John	--					
Cunningham	Lavina	--			Gobnascale	Donegal	1849	Garland	Derry

(*) See Endnotes

Last Name	First Name	Age	Family	Age	Address	County	Date	Ship	Port
Cunningham	Matilda	--			Ballymoney	Antrim	1850	Superior	Derry
Cunningham	Patt	30			Loughinisland	Down	1804	Commerce	--
Cunningham	Rebecca	--			L'Derry	Derry	1847	Venice	Derry
Curley	Patrick	20			Stewartstown	Tyrone	1803	Brutus	Derry
Curragan	Sarah	--			--	--	1811	Mary	Derry
Curran	William	--	John	--	Letterkenny	Donegal	1849	Envoy	Derry
Curren	Michael	--			Omagh	Tyrone	1850	Envoy	Derry
Curren	William	--			Dungiven	Derry	1848	MaryCampbell	Derry
Curry	Elizabeth	--			Coleraine	Derry	1849	Garland	Derry
Curry	Martha	--			Dungiven	Derry	1848	HannahKerr	Derry
Cuthbertson	Isabella	--			Fintona	Tyrone	1847	Hartford	Derry
Cuthbertson	Moses	--	Rebecca	--	Millford	Donegal	1847	Allegheny	Derry
Daley	Ann	--			Omagh	Tyrone	1847	Venice	Derry
Danford	Matty	--			Ture	Donegal	1850	Envoy	Derry
Darragh	Patrick	--	Peggy	--	Draperstown	Derry	1847	Venice	Derry
Darraghty	John	--			Dromore	(*)	1847	Montpellier	Derry
Davies	Margaret	--			Limavady	Derry	1850	Envoy	Derry
Davies	Robert	--	Margaret	--	Stranorlar	Donegal	1849	Envoy	Derry
Davis	Barnard	--			--	--	1811	Mary	Derry
Davis	James	--			Rosnakill	Donegal	1849	Superior	Derry
Davison	George	--	Ann	--	Letterkenny	Donegal	1847	Venice	Derry
Dawson	Sarah	17			Connor	Antrim	1803	George	Belfast
Dawson	William	28			--	--	1803	Edward	Belfast
Deeny	Sarah	--	Mary	--	Malin	Donegal	1849	Garland	Derry
Deery	James	--			Malin	Donegal	1848	MaryCampbell	Derry
Deery	John	--			Malin	Donegal	1850	Envoy	Derry
Deery	Mary	--	Rose	--	Ardmalin	Donegal	1847	Hartford	Derry
Deery	Michael	--	Mary	--	Malin	Donegal	1848	MaryCampbell	Derry
Deery	Unity	--			Ardmalin	Donegal	1847	Hartford	Derry
Delap	Samuel	--			Letterkenny	Donegal	1850	Superior	Derry
Denniston	WIlliam	--			Carrygalt	Donegal	1850	Superior	Derry
~Derin	Peter	56			Clanely	Tyrone	1803	Penna.	Derry
Develin	Roger	35	Jane	32	Ballymore	Armagh	1803	George	Belfast

(*) See Endnotes

Last Name	First Name	Age	Family	Age	Address	County	Date	Ship	Port
Devenny	Elinor	27			Killartie	Donegal	1804	Catherine	Bally- shannon
Devenny	Mary Ann	--			Coleraine	Derry	1849	Superior	Derry
Dever	Brigidt	55			Limavady	Derry	1803	Penna.	Derry
Dever	Fanny	--	Mary	10	Ballybofey	Donegal	1848	HannahKerr	Derry
Devilt	John	--			--	--	1811	Harmony	Derry
Devilt	Thomas	--			--	--	1811	Harmony	Derry
Devine	Ann	--			Fintona	Tyrone	1847	Allegheny	Derry
Devine	Catherine	--			Strabane	Tyrone	1847	Allegheny	Derry
Devine	John	--	Sarah	--	Lisdillon	Derry	1848	HannahKerr	Derry
Devine	John	30			Glack	Derry	1833-34	--	Derry
Devine	Mary	--	Daniel	11	--	--	1849	Garland	Derry
			Mary	9					
			Michael	7					
			Thomas	4					
			Robert	3m					
Devine	Michael	--	Margaret	--	Omagh	Tyrone	1847	Hershell	Derry
Devine	Neil	--			Dunnamanagh	Derry	1848	MaryCampbell	Derry
Devine	Thomas	--			Lisdillon	Derry	1848	HannahKerr	Derry
Devlin	Susanna	--			N'tnstewart	Tyrone	1847	Venice	Derry
Diamond	Mary	6	John	4	Terrydremont	Derry	1833-34	--	Derry
Dick	Thomas	32			--	Down	1803	Patty	Newry
Dickey	Isaac	20			Magheragill	Down	1804	Commerce	--
Dickey	James	--			--	--	1811	Fame	Derry
Dickey	Nathaniel	--			--	--	1811	Fame	Derry
Dickey	Samuel	--			--	--	1811	Fame	Derry
Dillon	Mary	--			L'Derry	Derry	1847	Montpellier	Derry
Dinsmore	Isabella	--			Prehen	Derry	1850	Superior	Derry
Dinwiddie	William	40			Dunaghy	Antrim	1804	Commerce	--
Divan	John	--	Catherine	--	Glenmore	(*)	1847	Allegheny	Derry
Diven	Pat	28			Strabane	Tyrone	1803	Mohawk	Derry
Diver	Matty	--			Ramelton	Donegal	1848	HannahKerr	Derry
Diver	Patrick	--			Dunfanaghy	Donegal	1848	HannahKerr	Derry

(*) See Endnotes

ULSTER EMIGRANTS TO PHILADELPHIA

Last Name	First Name	Age	Family	Age	Address	County	Date	Ship	Port
Diver	Sarah	--	Neill	10	Rathmullan	Donegal	1849	Garland	Derry
			Hugh	6					
Diver	Thomas	25			Fintragh	Donegal	1804	Jefferson	Bally-shannon
Divin	Nancy	--			Claudy	Derry	1849	Garland	Derry
Dixon	James	--	Charlotte	--	Millford	Donegal	1848	MaryCampbell	Derry
Dixon	Mary Ann	--			Churchtown	Donegal	1847	Hershell	Derry
Dixon	Robert	--			Fahan	Donegal	1847	Hershell	Derry
Doake	David	--			Omagh	Tyrone	1847	Montpellier	Derry
Dodds	John	30			Dromain	Antrim	1803	George	Belfast
Dogherty	James	51			--	--	1804	Maria	Derry
Dogherty	John	17			Drummond	Derry	1833-34	--	Derry
Doherty	Catherine	--			Clonmany	Donegal	1850	Lumley	Derry
Doherty	Catherine	--			L'Derry	Derry	1850	Envoy	Derry
Doherty	Charles	--			L'Derry	Derry	1850	Envoy	Derry
Doherty	Charles	--	Catherine	--	Clonmany	Donegal	1847	Superior	Derry
			Michael	--					
			Owen	--					
			Peggy	--					
Doherty	Edward	13	Catherine	11	Culdaff	Donegal	1848	HannahKerr	Derry
			Eleanor	9					
			Ann	7					
Doherty	Edward	25			Ballyscullion	Derry	1833-34	--	Derry
Doherty	Ellinah	--			Malin	Donegal	1850	Envoy	Derry
Doherty	Fanny	--	Roger	7	Ballygorman	Donegal	1849	Superior	Derry
			Rose	5					
Doherty	George	--			Ballybofey	Donegal	1848	HannahKerr	Derry
Doherty	George	--	Eliza	12	Ballybofey	Donegal	1848	HannahKerr	Derry
Doherty	George	--	Rebecca	--	Letterkenny	Donegal	1847	Venice	Derry
Doherty	Henry	--			L'Derry	Derry	1849	Superior	Derry
Doherty	James	--			Letterkenny	Donegal	1850	Superior	Derry
Doherty	James	28			Beefan	Donegal	1804	Brothers	Derry
Doherty	Jane	--	James	6	Strabane	Tyrone	1849	Garland	Derry
			John	9m					

Last Name	First Name	Age	Family	Age	Address	County	Date	Ship	Port
Doherty	John	--	Bridgit	--	Raphoe	Donegal	1847	Superior	Derry
			John	--					
			Catherine	--					
			Mary	7					
			Patrick	5					
			Biddy	3					
			James	1					
Doherty	John	--			Bann?	?	1849	Garland	Derry
Doherty	John	--			Carne	Donegal	1849	Envoy	Derry
Doherty	John	--			Rosses	Donegal	1849	Envoy	Derry
Doherty	John	--	Rosey	--	Glengivney	?	1847	Allegheny	Derry
			William	3					
			James	3m					
			Marg.Ann	4					
Doherty	John	30	Mary	26	Innishannon	Donegal	1804	Brothers	Derry
Doherty	Mandy	--			Rathmullan	Donegal	1847	Hartford	Derry
Doherty	Martha	--			Coleraine	Derry	1849	Superior	Derry
Doherty	Mary	--			Birdstown	Donegal	1849	Superior	Derry
Doherty	Mary	--			Malin	Donegal	1847	Hartford	Derry
Doherty	Michael	--			Rosnakill	Donegal	1849	Garland	Derry
Doherty	Michael	--	John	--	Coleraine	Derry	1850	Envoy	Derry
Doherty	Michael	24			Ballyscullion	Derry	1833-34	--	Derry
Doherty	Nancy	22			Upr. Drumons	Derry	1833-34	--	Derry
Doherty	Neal	--	Peggy	--	Ballybofey	Donegal	1848	HannahKerr	Derry
			Mary	--					
			Sally	--					
Doherty	Patrick	--			Culdaff	Donegal	1849	Envoy	Derry
Doherty	Patrick	--	Hugh	--	Rathmullan	Donegal	1847	Allegheny	Derry
Doherty	Patrick	--	John	--	Carndonagh	Donegal	1850	Envoy	Derry
			Catherine	--					
Doherty	Phillip	--	Patrick	--	Ballygorman	Donegal	1849	Superior	Derry
Doherty	Robert	--	Betty	--	Claudy	Derry	1847	Barbara	Derry
Doherty	Robert	--	Catherine	11	Kilmacrenan	Donegal	1847	MaryStewart	Derry
			Eliza	9					

Last Name	First Name	Age	Family	Age	Address	County	Date	Ship	Port
			(Cont'd.)						
			James	--					
Doherty	Sarah	--			Burt	Donegal	1847	Venice	Derry
Doherty	Sarah	--	Nancy	12	Castlederg	Tyrone	1847	Superior	Derry
			James	10					
			Samuel	8					
			Patrick	6					
			John	3					
			Hugh	1					
Doherty	William	--			Clondermott	Derry	1849	Superior	Derry
Doherty	William	--			Raphoe	Donegal	1847	Superior	Derry
Doherty	William	--			SixMileCross	Tyrone	1850	Superior	Derry
Doherty	William	--	Margaret	--	Castlefin	Donegal	1849	Garland	Derry
			Pat	--					
			Elleanor	--					
			Hugh	8					
			Mary	4					
Doherty	William	22			Ballyscullion	Derry	1833-34	--	Derry
Doherty	William	22	Edward	25	Ballyscullion	Derry	1833-34	--	Derry
Doherty	William	23			Innishannon	Donegal	1804	Brothers	Derry
Doherty	William	24			Ballymultimber	Derry	1833-34	--	Derry
Dolan	John	--	Catherine	--	Strabane	Tyrone	1847	Hartford	Derry
Donaghy	James	--	Mary	--	Learmount	Derry	1847	Hershell	Derry
Donaghy	James	11	MaryAnn	9	Dunnamanagh	Derry	1847	Barbara	Derry
Donaghy	John	--	Mary Ann	--	Beragh	Tyrone	1850	Superior	Derry
Donaghy	Patrick	--	Catherine	--	Clonmany	Donegal	1847	Superior	Derry
			Biddy	12					
			John	3					
			James	4					
			Ellen	2					
Donaghy	Peter	--	Margaret	--	Buncrana	Donegal	1847	Venice	Derry
			Peter	11					
			Henry	9					
			Bridget	--					

ULSTER EMIGRANTS TO PHILADELPHIA

Last Name	First Name	Age	Family	Age	Address	County	Date	Ship	Port
Donaghy	Rose	--			Knackan	Derry	1847	Montpellier	Derry
Donald	Patrick	50			Clanely	Tyrone	1803	Penna.	Derry
Donaldson	Mary	20			Clanely	Tyrone	1803	Penna.	Derry
Donaldson	Robert	46	Bell	36	Strabane	Tyrone	1803	Penna.	Derry
			Mary	24					
			Jane	5					
Donally	Edward	--			Gortin	(*)	1849	Garland	Derry
Donally	John	--	Mary	--	Ederny	Fermanagh	1847	Venice	Derry
Donan	Thomas	23			Taughblane	Down	1803	Mohawk	Derry
Donnel	Margaret	--			St.Johnstown	Donegal	1847	Venice	Derry
Donnell	Michael	--			Crossroads	Donegal	1847	Hartford	Derry
Donnell	Nancy	--			Clondermott	Derry	1850	Envoy	Derry
Donnelley	John	--			Beragh	Tyrone	1849	Superior	Derry
Donnelly	Edward	27			Lissan	Tyrone	1803	George	Belfast
Donnelly	Ellen	--	William	--	Ballybofey	Donegal	1848	HannahKerr	Derry
			Beranrd	10					
			Margaret	8					
			Ann	6					
			Catherine	4					
			Hugh	2					
Donnelly	James	--			Draperstown	Derry	1850	Superior	Derry
Donnelly	John	--			Draperstown	Derry	1847	Venice	Derry
Donnelly	Matilda	--			Coleraine	Derry	1848	HannahKerr	Derry
Donnelly	Mick	--			Beragh	Tyrone	1847	Montpellier	Derry
Donnelly	Rose	--			Plumbridge	Derry	1847	Superior	Derry
Donohoe	James	--	Margaret	--	Lisdillon	Derry	1848	HannahKerr	Derry
Donohoe	Mary Ann	--			Lisdillon	Derry	1848	HannahKerr	Derry
Doran	James	--			Rosnakill	Donegal	1850	Envoy	Derry
Doran	Thomas	--	Catherine	--	Lowtherstown	Fermanagh	1847	Hartford	Derry
			Mary	--					
			Mary	7					
			Sarah	4					
			Margaret	2					

(*) See Endnotes

ULSTER EMIGRANTS TO PHILADELPHIA

Last Name	First Name	Age	Family	Age	Address	County	Date	Ship	Port
Dormet	Francis	20			L'Derry	Derry	1803	Penna.	Derry
Douds	Mary	--	Elleanor	--	Killea	Derry	1848	MaryCampbell	Derry
			John	--					
Dougherty	Ann	--			L'Derry	Derry	1847	Montpellier	Derry
Dougherty	Bridget	--	Margaret	--	Fahan	Donegal	1847	Superior	Derry
Dougherty	Darby	25			Ardmalin	Donegal	1803	Mohawk	Derry
Dougherty	Edward	--			Glentogher	Donegal	1849	Envoy	Derry
Dougherty	Ellen	--	Ellen	--	Buncrana	Donegal	1849	Envoy	Derry
Dougherty	Henry	--	Catherine	--	--	--	1811	Harmony	Derry
			Anthony	--					
Dougherty	James	--			Kilmacrenan	Donegal	1850	Envoy	Derry
Dougherty	James	33			--	--	1804	Maria	Derry
Dougherty	John	--	Michael	--	Malin	Donegal	1850	Superior	Derry
Dougherty	Margaret	--			Limavady	Derry	1850	Envoy	Derry
Dougherty	Margaret	--	Patrick	5	Cookstown	Tyrone	1848	MaryCampbell	Derry
			Michael	3					
Dougherty	Mary	--	James	2	Malin	Donegal	1850	Superior	Derry
			Nancy	6m					
Dougherty	Neal	20			Buncrana	Donegal	1803	Mohawk	Derry
Dougherty	Richard	36			Tullaghan	Donegal	1803	Penna.	Derry
Dougherty	Thomas	--	Abigale	--	--	--	1811	Mary	Derry
Douglass	John	38	Mary	38	Seaford	Down	1804	Commerce	--
Douglass	Joseph	--			--	--	1811	Mary	Derry
Douglass	Matthew	21			Largyreagh	Derry	1833-34	--	Derry
Doutherd	Hannah	--			Ballybofey	Donegal	1848	HannahKerr	Derry
Douthwit	Thomas	--	Jane	--	Letterkenny	Donegal	1849	Envoy	Derry
Douthwitt	Stephen	--			Letterkenny	Donegal	1847	Hershell	Derry
Dowds	Catherine	--			Killea	Derry	1848	MaryCampbell	Derry
Downing	Hugh	--			Kesh	Fermanagh	1849	Garland	Derry
Doyle	Catherine	--			--	--	1811	Mary	Derry
Drew	George	--	Nancy	--	Stranorlar	Donegal	1847	Allegheny	Derry
			Jane	--					
Drum	Thomas	36	Nathaniel	34	Enniskillen	Fermanagh	1803	Mohawk	Derry
Drum	William	20	Mary	16	Enniskillen	Fermanagh	1803	Mohawk	Derry

24

Last Name	First Name	Age	Family	Age	Address	County	Date	Ship	Port
Dudgeon	Robert	--			Dunfanaghy	Donegal	1849	Garland	Derry
Duffin	John	--	Catherine	--	Cookstown	Tyrone	1848	MaryCampbell	Derry
			Jane	9					
			Charles	7					
			James	6					
			Sarah	4					
Duffy	Bridget	--	Mary	11	Churchill	Donegal	1847	Hartford	Derry
Duffy	Catherine	--			Ramelton	Donegal	1849	Superior	Derry
Duffy	Mary	--	Sally	--	Ramelton	Donegal	1847	Hershell	Derry
Duffy	Michael	--	Nancy	--	Draperstown	Derry	1847	Superior	Derry
Duffy	William	--			Muff	Derry	1849	Superior	Derry
Dugan	Farrigle	--			Creeslough	Donegal	1847	MaryStewart	Derry
Dugan	John	--			Clougheneely	Donegal	1847	Venice	Derry
Duncan	James	--			Baronscourt	Tyrone	1847	Barbara	Derry
Duncan	Margaret	--			--	--	1811	Mary	Derry
Dunlop	Jane	--	Thomas	10	Cookstown	Tyrone	1847	Allegheny	Derry
			Sarah	6					
			John	2					
Dunlop	Samuel	--	Mary	--	Carrigans	Donegal	1847	Hartford	Derry
			Mary	9m					
Dunn	Adm.	30			--	--	1803	Edward	Belfast
Dunn	Charles	--	Patrick	12	Strabane	Tyrone	1850	Envoy	Derry
Dunn	James	24	Mary	19	Beefan	Donegal	1804	Brothers	Derry
Durnin	Margaret	--	Mary	9	Dunfanaghy	Donegal	1847	Superior	Derry
			Charles	6					
Duross	John	21			--	Dublin	1804	Commerce	--
Eakin	Alex.	26			Terrydremont	Derry	1833-34	--	Derry
Eakin	Alexander	28			Coleraine	Derry	1803	Brutus	Derry
Earley	Ann	--			Ballygawley	(*)	1850	Envoy	Derry
Eaton	Robert	--			Castlederg	Tyrone	1849	Envoy	Derry
Edmond	William	41			--	--	1804	Maria	Derry
Edmondon	James	--			--	--	1811	Mary	Derry
Edwards	Isabella	--			Stranorlar	Donegal	1849	Envoy	Derry

(*) See Endnotes

Last Name	First Name	Age	Family	Age	Address	County	Date	Ship	Port
Egan	Peter	--	Margaret	--	Omagh	Tyrone	1850	Envoy	Derry
			Eliza	--					
Eglinton	Samuel	--			Glenfin	Roscommon	1850	Superior	Derry
Elder	William	--			Letterkenny	Donegal	1849	Envoy	Derry
Elgin	James	10			St.Johnston	Donegal	1803	Penna.	Derry
Elkin	William	--			Omagh	Tyrone	1850	Superior	Derry
Elliot	Hamilton	--	Nancy	--	Strabane	Tyrone	1847	Allegheny	Derry
			Margaret	--					
			William	10					
			Thomas	8					
			Andrew	6					
			Hamilton	4					
Eskin	Samuel	50	James	46	--	Down	1803	Patty	Newry
Etherston	Ellen	--			Moville	Donegal	1850	Superior	Derry
Ewing	Ann	--			Letterkenny	Donegal	1849	Superior	Derry
Ewing	John	20			L'Derry	Derry	1803	Brutus	Derry
Ewing	Joseph	--	Jane	--	Ture	Donegal	1850	Envoy	Derry
			Alex	--					
Ewing	Rebecca	--			Ture	Donegal	1850	Envoy	Derry
Ewing	William	--			N'tncunningham	Donegal	1847	Hershell	Derry
Faggart	Samuel	30	Margaret	28	Clones	Monaghan	1803	Mohawk	Derry
Fairman	Robert	--			Convoy	Donegal	1849	Envoy	Derry
Faith	Nancy	--			Garvagh	Derry	1847	Hartford	Derry
Farran	Elleanonr	--			Culdaff	Donegal	1848	HannahKerr	Derry
Farran	Peggy	--			Culdaff	Donegal	1848	HannahKerr	Derry
Fawcet	Arthur	19			Lochris	Donegal	1804	Catherine	Bally-shannon
Fawcett	Catherine	21			Drumhome	Donegal	1804	Catherine	Bally-shannon
Fee	James	--			--	--	1811	Mary	Derry
Fee	Mary	--	Ann	12	Fintona	Tyrone	1847	Allegheny	Derry
			Sarah	10					
Fee	Patrick	--			--	--	1811	Mary	Derry
Feeny	John	--	Mary	--	Claudy	Derry	1847	Montpellier	Derry

ULSTER EMIGRANTS TO PHILADELPHIA

Last Name	First Name	Age	Family	Age	Address	County	Date	Ship	Port
Ferguson	David	--			Gorticross	Derry	1850	Envoy	Derry
Ferguson	William	--			Limavady	Derry	1847	Allegheny	Derry
Ferrier	James	24			Bushmills	Antrim	1803	Brutus	Derry
Ferris	Daniel	--			Limavady	Derry	1849	Garland	Derry
Ferris	William	25	Ann	32	Ballymena	Antrim	1804	Commerce	--
Ferry	Catherine	--			Letterkenny	Donegal	1847	Venice	Derry
Ferry	John	--			Crossroads	Donegal	1847	Montpellier	Derry
Ferry	John	--	Catherine	--	Crossroads	Donegal	1850	Envoy	Derry
Ferry	William	--			L'Derry	Derry	1847	Hershell	Derry
Ferson	William	24			Ballymultimber	Derry	1833-34	--	Derry
Fife	James	--			--	--	1811	Mary	Derry
Findlay	Rachel	--	Jane	--	Coleraine	Derry	1847	Venice	Derry
Finlay	Andrew	--			Raphoe	Donegal	1847	Montpellier	Derry
Fisher	Abigale	--			L'Derry	Derry	1850	Superior	Derry
Fisher	George	--			Ramelton	Donegal	1847	Hershell	Derry
Fisher	Margaret	--	Ruth	--	Ramelton	Donegal	1849	Garland	Derry
Fisher	Martha	--	Martha	--	Ballybofey	Donegal	1848	HannahKerr	Derry
			James	10					
			Margaret	8					
			Samuel	6					
			John	--					
Fisher	Samuel	--			Letterkenny	Donegal	1847	Superior	Derry
Fitspatrick	James	37			--	Down	1803	Patty	Newry
Fitspatrick	Mary	32			--	Down	1803	Patty	Newry
Flanagan	John	--	Mary	--	Letterkenny	Donegal	1847	Venice	Derry
Flanagan	Patrick	--			--	--	1811	Mary	Derry
Flanaghan	Peter	--			Ballygawley	Tyrone	1849	Garland	Derry
Flanigan	Charles	34	Mary	28	Ballyshannon	Donegal	1804	Brothers	Derry
			Jno.	6					
Fleming	John	24			--	Queens	1803	Patty	Newry
Flemming	Henry	--			Limavady	Derry	1847	Allegheny	Derry
Flemming	James	--			Limavady	Derry	1847	Allegheny	Derry
Flemming	Mary Ann	--	Franci	--	Churchill	Donegal	1847	Hartford	Derry
Flemming	Samuel	--			Ballybofey	Donegal	1848	HannahKerr	Derry

ULSTER EMIGRANTS TO PHILADELPHIA

Last Name	First Name	Age	Family	Age	Address	County	Date	Ship	Port
Flemming	Thomas	--	William	--	Ballybofey	Donegal	1848	HannahKerr	Derry
Flemming	Thomas	19			--	--	1803	Edward	Belfast
Flinn	James	--			Pettigoe	(*)	1849	Superior	Derry
Flynn	Hugh	--	Catherine	--	Kesh	Fermanagh	1847	Montpellier	Derry
			Isabella	11					
			John	9					
			Jane	6					
			Catherine	2					
Folhall	Laurin	--			--	--	1811	Mary	Derry
Forrest	Daniel	--			Churchill	Donegal	1849	Superior	Derry
Forrest	Esther	--	Eliza	12	N'tncunningham	Donegal	1847	Venice	Derry
			MaryJane	11					
			Rachel	7					
			Aly	6					
Forrester	Henry	24			Clones	Monaghan	1803	Mohawk	Derry
Fox	James	40			--	--	1803	Edward	Belfast
Frame	Thomas	--	Margaret	--	Strabane	Tyrone	1847	MaryStewart	Derry
Freel	Mary	--			Garvagh	Derry	1847	Venice	Derry
Friel	Charles	--	Isabella	--	Moville	Donegal	1847	Hartford	Derry
			Ellen	11					
Friel	John	--			Fanad	Donegal	1847	Venice	Derry
Friel	Manus	--	Bridget	--	Letterkenny	Donegal	1849	Envoy	Derry
Friel	Michael	--			Rosnakill	Donegal	1847	MaryStewart	Derry
Fullerton	Mary Jane	--			Coleraine	Derry	1850	Lumley	Derry
Fulton	Alexander	34			Loughill	Antrim	1803	George	Belfast
Fulton	Margaret	--	James	9	Portglenone	Antrim	1848	MaryCampbell	Derry
			Margarert	7					
			William	5					
			Rosanna	3					
			Nancy	1					

(*) See Endnotes

ULSTER EMIGRANTS TO PHILADELPHIA

Last Name	First Name	Age	Family	Age	Address	County	Date	Ship	Port
Fulton	Margaret	18	Samuel	14	Ballyclough	Derry	1833-34	--	Derry
			James	12					
			MaryAnn	10					
			Thomas	8					
Fulton	Nancy	31			--	--	1804	Maria	Derry
Fulton	Robert	43			--	--	1804	Maria	Derry
Gably	Hugh	18			Killinchy	Down	1803	George	Belfast
Gailey	Charles	--	Margaret	--	Letterkenny	Donegal	1847	Hartford	Derry
Gaileys ?					Ballybofey	Donegal	1848	HannahKerr	Derry
Gallagher	Bridget	--	John	7	Letterkenny	Donegal	1847	Montpellier	Derry
			Bridget	5					
Gallagher	Catherine	--			Strabane	Tyrone	1847	Allegheny	Derry
Gallagher	Charles	--			--	--	1811	Harmony	Derry
Gallagher	Daniel	--			Creeslough	Donegal	1847	MaryStewart	Derry
Gallagher	Daniel	--			Crossroads	Donegal	1847	Montpellier	Derry
Gallagher	Daniel	--			Gortahork	Donegal	1847	Hershell	Derry
Gallagher	Dennis	--			Clougheneely	Donegal	1849	Superior	Derry
Gallagher	Elizabeth	--	Fanny	--	Kesh	Fermanagh	1850	Superior	Derry
Gallagher	Fanny	--	Mary	--	Letterkenny	Donegal	1847	MaryStewart	Derry
Gallagher	George	--			Fanad	Donegal	1847	Superior	Derry
Gallagher	George	--			Millford	Donegal	1848	MaryCampbell	Derry
Gallagher	Giles	--	Mary	12	Carrygalt	Donegal	1847	Venice	Derry
			John	4					
			Nancy	1					
Gallagher	James	--	Ann	--	Rathmullan	Donegal	1849	Superior	Derry
			Patrick	3m					
Gallagher	James	--	Catherine	--	Castlefin	Donegal	1848	HannahKerr	Derry
			John	9					
			James	7					
			Biddy	4					
			Hugh	2					
Gallagher	James	--	Mary	--	Killeter	Tyrone	1850	Superior	Derry
			William	10					
			Hugh	8					

ULSTER EMIGRANTS TO PHILADELPHIA

Last Name	First Name	Age	Family	Age	Address	County	Date	Ship	Port
(Cont'd.)			Elizabeth	6					
			Mary	4					
Gallagher	James	--	Mary	--	Ramelton	Donegal	1847	Hershell	Derry
			James	--					
			William	--					
			Robert	--					
			Mary	9					
			Mathew	5					
			Fanny	2					
Gallagher	John	--			Kilmacrenan	Donegal	1847	MaryStewart	Derry
Gallagher	John	--	Margaret	--	Waterside	Derry	1847	Venice	Derry
Gallagher	Letitia	--			Ramelton	Donegal	1847	Hartford	Derry
Gallagher	Mary	--			Whitecastle	Donegal	1850	Superior	Derry
Gallagher	Mary	--	Catherine	--	--	--	1811	Harmony	Derry
			Patrick	--					
			Michael	--					
			Hugh	--					
Gallagher	Mary Ann	--			Pettigoe	(*)	1849	Garland	Derry
Gallagher	Michael	--			Draperstown	Derry	1847	Superior	Derry
Gallagher	Neal	--			Letterkenny	Donegal	1850	Envoy	Derry
Gallagher	Peggy	--	Paddy	--	Clougheneely	Donegal	1847	Venice	Derry
Gallagher	Robert	--	Charles	--	Ramelton	Donegal	1850	Envoy	Derry
Gallagher	William	--			Raphoe	Donegal	1850	Superior	Derry
Gallen	Hugh	--	Mary	--	--	--	1811	Harmony	Derry
			Margaret	--					
			Owen	--					
			Sally	--					
			Biddy	--					
			Mary	--					
			James	--					
			Catherine	--					
Gallmagh	Nancy	--	Ann	--	Ballybofey	Donegal	1848	HannahKerr	Derry
Gallon	Michael	--			Banagher	Fermanagh	1847	Superior	Derry

(*) See Endnotes

30

ULSTER EMIGRANTS TO PHILADELPHIA

Last Name	First Name	Age	Family	Age	Address	County	Date	Ship	Port
Gallon	Patrick	--	Mary	--	Killygordon	(*)	1847	Barbara	Derry
			Margaret	5					
			Mary	9m					
Gamble	Elizabeth	--	Joseph	8	Craig	(*)	1849	Garland	Derry
Gamble	Jane	--	Elizabeth	--	Ballybofey	Donegal	1848	HannahKerr	Derry
			William	5					
			Sarah	2					
Gamble	Mary	--			Coleraine	Derry	1850	Lumley	Derry
Gamble	Robert	--			Craig	(*)	1847	Barbara	Derry
Gamble	Sarah	--			Craig	(*)	1847	Barbara	Derry
Ganet	James	30			Annahilt	Down	1803	George	Belfast
Gardener	James	--			Coleraine	Derry	1847	MaryStewart	Derry
Gardner	Mary	--			Omagh	Tyrone	1850	Envoy	Derry
Gaston	Anna	--			Strabane	Tyrone	1847	Barbara	Derry
Gault	Mary	--			Ballybofey	Donegal	1848	HannahKerr	Derry
Genagal	Mary	--			--	--	1811	Mary	Derry
George	Adam	--			--	--	1811	Fame	Derry
George	Alex.	21			Terrydremont	Derry	1833-34	--	Derry
George	John	--			--	--	1811	Harmony	Derry
Getty	Arthur	--			Ballybofey	Donegal	1848	HannahKerr	Derry
Getty	Joseph	20	Martha	--	Largy	Derry	1833-34	--Derry	
Geurly	Jane	--			Letterkenny	Donegal	1849	Envoy	Derry
Gibbons	Charles	--			Letterkenny	Donegal	1849	Envoy	Derry
Gibbons	William	--	Rose	--	Letterkenny	Donegal	1847	Barbara	Derry
			James	12					
			Ellen	6					
			Julia	4					
			Neil	2					
Gibson	Andrew	--			--	--	1811	Mary	Derry
Gibson	Jane	--	Hannah	--	St.Johnstown	Donegal	1847	Venice	Derry
Gibson	John	--	Mary	--	Beragh	Tyrone	1847	Hartford	Derry
Gibson	John	50	--			Tyrone	1803	Patty	Newry

(*) See Endnotes

31

ULSTER EMIGRANTS TO PHILADELPHIA

Last Name	First Name	Age	Family	Age	Address	County	Date	Ship	Port
Gilfillan	Margaret	--			Raphoe	Donegal	1850	Superior	Derry
Gill	Patrick	--			Burnfoot	Donegal	1849	Superior	Derry
Gillespie	James	--			--	--	1811	Mary	Derry
Gillespie	James	--			Gidore ?	?	1847	Hartford	Derry
Gillespie	James	--	John	--	Coleraine	Derry	1849	Superior	Derry
Gillespie	William	--			Waterside	Derry	1849	Superior	Derry
Gillespy	Patt	35	Peggy	24	Glen	Donegal	1804	Catherine	Bally-shannon
Gills	Joseph	--			Birdstown	Donegal	1848	HannahKerr	Derry
Gilmour	James	--	Ann	15	Beragh	Tyrone	1847	Superior	Derry
Gilmour	John	--			--	--	1811	Harmony	Derry
Gilmour	Samuel	20			St.Johnston	Donegal	1803	Penna.	Derry
Given	Thomas	--			Limavady	Derry	1849	Garland	Derry
Glackin	William	--			Malin	Donegal	1849	Superior	Derry
Glass	Andrew	--	Martha	--	Drumquin	Tyrone	1847	Superior	Derry
			Alexander	11					
			Edward	10					
			Samuel	7					
			Margaret	5					
			Andrew	2					
Glen	Jane	--			Coleraine	Derry	1849	Superior	Derry
Glen	Robert	--			Coleraine	Derry	1849	Envoy	Derry
Glen	Samuel	--			--	--	1811	Mary	Derry
Glenn	James	--			Coleraine	Derry	1849	Garland	Derry
Glin	William	25			Letterkenny	Donegal	1803	Mohawk	Derry
Godfrey	George	--			Newbuildings	(*)	1847	Montpellier	Derry
Gordan	Mary Ann	--	Elleanor	--	Strabane	Tyrone	1848	MaryCampbell	Derry
Gordon	Jane	--			Ballymoney	Antrim	1849	Superior	Derry
Gordon	John	--			--	--	1811	Harmony	Derry
Gordon	John	36			Keady	Armagh	1804	Commerce	--
Gordon	William	--			Ballsallagh	Antrim	1847	Allegheny	Derry
Gorman	Bridget	--			Gortin	(*)	1847	Montpellier	Derry

(*) See Endnotes

32

ULSTER EMIGRANTS TO PHILADELPHIA

Last Name	First Name	Age	Family	Age	Address	County	Date	Ship	Port
Gormley	Henry	--			Coleraine	Derry	1847	Allegheny	Derry
Gormly	Francis	--			Omagh	Tyrone	1848	MaryCampbell	Derry
Gormly	Patrick	--	Mick	--	Castlederg	Tyrone	1848	MaryCampbell	Derry
Gormly	Roseanna	--			Strabane	Tyrone	1850	Superior	Derry
Gormly	Sarah	--	Margaret	--	Gallagh	Antrim	1849	Garland	Derry
Gormly	William	--			Lowtherstown	Fermanagh	1849	Garland	Derry
Graham	Elizabeth	--	Rebecca	--	Omagh	Tyrone	1850	Superior	Derry
Graham	Humphry	50			--	--	1804	Maria	Derry
Graham	Margaret	--	Mary	7	Kilmacrenan	Donegal	1847	MaryStewart	Derry
			John	5					
			Joseph	3					
			Isabella	1					
Graham	Mary	--			Strabane	Tyrone	1847	Montpellier	Derry
Graham	Robert	20			Bolea	Derry	1803	Mohawk	Derry
Graham	Thomas	--	Mary	--	Tempo	Fermanagh	1847	Barbara	Derry
			William	--					
Graham	Thomas	36			--	--	1804	Maria	Derry
Gray	John	--	James	--	Gortin	(*)	1847	Superior	Derry
			ElizaJane	--					
			John	3					
			William	3m					
Gray	Joseph	--	Susan	--	Coleraine	Derry	1849	Superior	Derry
Gray	Mary	--			Moneymore	(*)	1847	Venice	Derry
Gray	William	24			--	Tyrone	1803	Strafford	Derry
Green	Dennis	--	Catherine	--	Killygordon	(*)	1847	Barbara	Derry
			Sarah	6					
			Michael	4					
			Hugh	2					
Green	Eliza	--			Killygordon	(*)	1847	Barbara	Derry
Green	John	--			Fanad	Donegal	1847	Superior	Derry
Greer	ELizabeth	--			Castlederg	Tyrone	1849	Superior	Derry
Greer	James	--			Carrygalt	Donegal	1850	Lumley	Derry

(*) See Endnotes

ULSTER EMIGRANTS TO PHILADELPHIA

Last Name	First Name	Age	Family	Age	Address	County	Date	Ship	Port
Greer	Marcus	--	Keatty	--	L'Derry	Derry	1850	Envoy	Derry
			Adam	--					
Greer	Margaret	--			Dunfanaghy	Donegal	1850	Lumley	Derry
Greer	Matty	--			Churchill	Donegal	1847	Hartford	Derry
Greer	Robert	--	JaneMary	--	Carrygalt	Donegal	1850	Envoy	Derry
Greg	James	46	Thomas	18	--	--	1803	Edward	Belfast
			John	19					
Gregg	Margaret	--			Ballymoney	Antrim	1850	Lumley	Derry
Grey	Margaret	--			Ballybofey	Donegal	1848	HannahKerr	Derry
Grier	Thomas	30	Jane	23	Drumhome	Donegal	1804	Catherine	Bally-shannon
Griffeth	Rose	--	Biddy	--	--	--	1811	Harmony	Derry
Griffis	William	34			--	Down	1803	Patty	Newry
Griffith	Archibald	--	Hannah	--	Gobnascale	Donegal	1849	Garland	Derry
Griffith	John	--			Killygordon	(*)	1850	Superior	Derry
Grimes	James	--			--	--	1811	Fame	Derry
Grissum	Jasper	--	Sarah	--	Garvagh	Derry	1848	MaryCampbell	Derry
Groves	George	--	Nancy	--	Ramelton	Donegal	1848	HannahKerr	Derry
			Edward	11					
			Catherine	6					
			Mary	4					
Groves	George	--	Thomas	--	Ramelton	Donegal	1847	Venice	Derry
Gwyn	David	--	Margaret	--	Lifford	(*)	1849	Envoy	Derry
			Thomas	--					
			Margaret	--					
			MaryJane	13					
			Isabella	8					
			David	3					
Hackett	Michael	--			Beragh	Tyrone	1848	MaryCampbell	Derry
Haddock	Joseph	27			--	--	1803	Edward	Belfast
Hagan	Pat	--			Draperstown	Derry	1850	Superior	Derry
Hagerty	Thomas	--			Glenties	Donegal	1849	Superior	Derry

(*) See Endnotes

ULSTER EMIGRANTS TO PHILADELPHIA

Last Name	First Name	Age	Family	Age	Address	County	Date	Ship	Port
Hamill	John	--			--	--	1811	Harmony	Derry
Hamilton	Charles	--	Daniel	--	--	--	1811	Mary	Derry
Hamilton	James	--			Ardstraw	Tyrone	1850	Envoy	Derry
Hamilton	James	23			Loughlin	Donegal	1803	Strafford	Derry
Hamilton	Robert	--			--	--	1811	Harmony	Derry
Hamilton	Robert	--	Mary	--	Limavady	Derry	1847	MaryStewart	Derry
Hamilton	William	--			--	--	1811	Mary	Derry
Hammond	Mary Ann	27			--	--	1804	Maria	Derry
Haney	Ann	--	Ellen	--	Claudy	Derry	1847	Montpellier	Derry
Haney	James	--			Claudy	Derry	1847	Montpellier	Derry
Haney	Susan	--			Claudy	Derry	1847	Montpellier	Derry
Hanlan	John	--			--	--	1811	Harmony	Derry
Hanlan	Thomas	--			Ramelton	Donegal	1847	Montpellier	Derry
Hanlay	Ardsal	22			--	--	1803	Edward	Belfast
Hanlen	Patrick	--			Ramelton	Donegal	1850	Envoy	Derry
Hanley	Daniel	--			Ramelton	Donegal	1849	Envoy	Derry
Harkin	Barney	--			Moville	Donegal	1847	Hartford	Derry
Harkin	Catherine	--			Dunfanaghy	Donegal	1849	Superior	Derry
Harkin	Charles	--			Dunfanaghy	Donegal	1847	Hershell	Derry
Harkin	Keatty	--			Clonmany	Donegal	1849	Superior	Derry
Harkin	Nancy	30	William	6	Birdstown	Donegal	1803	Strafford	Derry
			Nelly	4					
Harkin	Owen	--			Clonmany	Donegal	1850	Lumley	Derry
Harkin	Pat	--			Clonmany	Donegal	1847	Superior	Derry
Harkin	William	25			--	--	1804	Maria	Derry
Harley	Catherine	--			Fanad	Donegal	1847	Hershell	Derry
Harran	Susan	--			Castlederg	Tyrone	1849	Garland	Derry
Harran	William	37	Elizabeth	37	Drumhome	Donegal	1804	Catherine	Bally-shannon
			Ann	13					
			Jane	13					
			John	10					
			Alexander	7					

ULSTER EMIGRANTS TO PHILADELPHIA

Last Name	First Name	Age	Family	Age	Address	County	Date	Ship	Port
Harran	William	37	Jane	32	Drumhome	Donegal	1804	Catherine	Bally-
			Barbara	11					shannon
			Jane	8					
Harris	Margaret	--	Catherine	--	Letterkenny	Donegal	1847	Hartford	Derry
Harrity	Mary	--			Cross Roads	Donegal	1847	Hershell	Derry
Harrity	John	--			L'Derry	Derry	1849	Superior	Derry
Harrowdin	William	--	Sarah	--	Castlederg	Tyrone	1847	Venice	Derry
			Susan	7					
			Sarah	5					
			Margaret	1					
Hart	Sarah	--	Sarah	--	L'Derry	Derry	1850	Superior	Derry
Hartin	Edward	--			Carnaghan	Donegal	1850	Envoy	Derry
Harvey	David	--			--	--	1811	Mary	Derry
Harvey	Mary	45	Elizabeth	23	--	Armagh	1803	Patty	Newry
Harvey	Robert	48			--	Armagh	1803	Patty	Newry
Haslett	John	--			Dunfanaghy	Donegal	1847	Superior	Derry
Hassan	Roseann	--			Moville	Donegal	1850	Envoy	Derry
Hasson	John	24			Cumber	Derry	1803	Brutus	Derry
Hastings	John	--			Carrick	Donegal	1847	Hartford	Derry
Hastings	John	21			Stewartstown	Tyrone	1803	Mohawk	Derry
Hastings	Robert	--			Kilmacrenan	Donegal	1850	Lumley	Derry
Hatrick	Ellen	--			L'Derry	Derry	1850	Envoy	Derry
Hawks	George	--	Isabella	--	Omagh	Tyrone	1847	Superior	Derry
			Eliza	--					
			MaryAnn	11					
			George	10					
			Isabella	6					
			John	4					
			William	2					
			Martha	3m					
Hay	Hugh	--			Ramelton	Donegal	1849	Garland	Derry
Hayborn	Hannah	--			Omagh	Tyrone	1850	Envoy	Derry
Hazlett	Charles	35			Bogtown	Derry	1833	--	Derry

Last Name	First Name	Age	Family	Age	Address	County	Date	Ship	Port
Hearney	Ann	23	Patrick	12	Dungiven	Derry	1804	Brothers	Derry
			John	9					
			Biddy	7					
			Nanny	4					
Heaton	Margaret	28			Tullaghan	Donegal	1803	Penna.	Derry
Hector	Robert	--			--	--	1811	Fame	Derry
Hegarty	James	--	Biddy	--	Buncrana	Donegal	1849	Superior	Derry
Hegarty	John	--			L'Derry	Derry	1847	Montpellier	Derry
Hemphill	Hugh	27			Ballybritain	Derry	1833-34	--	Derry
Hemphill	MaryJane	--			Coleraine	Derry	1847	Venice	Derry
Hemphill	Sarah	--			Coleraine	Derry	1849	Superior	Derry
Henderson	David	--			Donaghadee	Down	1847	Venice	Derry
Henderson	Robert	45	Elenor	44	Lochris	Donegal	1804	Catherine	Bally-shannon
			Elenor	18					
			Jane	15					
			Prudence	13					
			George	11					
			Ann	8					
			Alexander	6					
Henderson	Sarah	--			L'Derry	Derry	1849	Superior	Derry
Henderson	Thomas	--			Castlederg	Tyrone	1849	Envoy	Derry
Henery	Robert	22			Lisboy	Derry	1833-34	--	Derry
Heney	Matilda	--			Cookstown	Tyrone	1850	Superior	Derry
Henry	Betty	--	Mathew	--	Draperstown	Derry	1850	Envoy	Derry
Henry	Catherine	--	Ann Jane	--	Maghera	Donegal	1849	Garland	Derry
			John	13					
			Mick	11					
			Arthur	9					
			David	7					
Henry	Molly	40			Termaquin	Derry	1833-34	--	Derry
Henry	William	--	Catherine	--	Magherafelt	Derry	1849	Garland	Derry
			Patrick	--					
			Margaret	6					
			Eliza	5					

ULSTER EMIGRANTS TO PHILADELPHIA

Last Name	First Name	Age	Family	Age	Address	County	Date	Ship	Port
Henry	William	--	Charlotte	--	Coleraine	Derry	1848	HannahKerr	Derry
Heraughty	Susan	--			Letterkenny	Donegal	1849	Garland	Derry
Heron	James	--			Millford	Donegal	1848	MaryCampbell	Derry
Hethrington	Charles	40	Susan	40	Dungannon	Tyrone	1803	Mohawk	Derry
			Josh	14					
			Elizabeth	16					
			George	10					
Hethrington	Christy	36			Dungannon	Tyrone	1803	Mohawk	Derry
Hewitt	John	--			Donegal	Donegal	1849	Envoy	Derry
Hibran	J.	30	Joseph	23	Castlefin	Donegal	1804	Brothers	Derry
Higgins	Patrick	--			Ballymoney	Antrim	1849	Garland	Derry
Hillard	James	--			Convoy	Donegal	1849	Superior	Derry
Hilley	James	--	Hugh	--	Ballintra	Donegal	1847	Hartford	Derry
			Ellan	--					
			Mary	--					
Himton	Jane	35			Castlefin	Donegal	1804	Brothers	Derry
Hoan	Hugh	--			Gowshill	Tyrone	1847	Allegheny	Derry
Holland	Rose	--			Ballybofey	Donegal	1848	HannahKerr	Derry
Honetin	Keatty	--			Stranorlar	Donegal	1850	Envoy	Derry
Hoot	Catherine	--			Strabane	Tyrone	1850	Envoy	Derry
Hopkin	Thomas	--	Jane (W)	--	Claudy	Derry	1847	Barbara	Derry
			Matilda	--					
			Ann	3m					
Hopkins	Robert	21			Bolea	Derry	1803	Mohawk	Derry
Hottan	Alice	--	Margaret	11	Fintona	Tyrone	1847	Barbara	Derry
Houlton	Margaret	--	Mary	--	Ballygawley	(*)	1849	Envoy	Derry
			Thomas	8					
			John	6					
			Patrick	5					
Houston	Alexander	45			Dungiven	Derry	1803	Penna.	Derry
Houston	Ellen	--			Culdaff	Donegal	1849	Superior	Derry
Houston	Francis	20			Dungiven	Derry	1803	Penna.	Derry

(*) See Endnotes

ULSTER EMIGRANTS TO PHILADELPHIA

Last Name	First Name	Age	Family	Age	Address	County	Date	Ship	Port
Houstone	Jane	--			Plumbridge	Derry	1847	Superior	Derry
Houten	James	--			Carne	Donegal	1847	Hartford	Derry
Hughes	Alexander	--			Emyvale	Monaghan	1849	Envoy	Derry
Hull	John	--			Garvagh	Derry	1848	MaryCampbell	Derry
Hunter	David	28			--	Tyrone	1803	Patty	Newry
Hunter	Edward	34	George	14	--	Tyrone	1803	Patty	Newry
Hunter	Eleanor	--			--	--	1811	Mary	Derry
Hunter	Gerard	--	Martha	--	--	--	1811	Harmony	Derry
			John	--					
			Mary	--					
Hunter	James	--	William	--	--	--	1811	Mary	Derry
Hunter	Mary Ann	--			Coleraine	Derry	1849	Superior	Derry
Hunter	Moses	--			--	--	1811	Fame	Derry
Hunter	Scott	--	Elizabeth	--	Limavady	Derry	1847	Venice	Derry
			Robert	8					
			William	6					
			John	6m					
Hunter	Scott	26			Tarnakelly	Derry	1833-34	--	Derry
Hurley	Mary	19			Coleraine	Derry	1833	--	Derry
Hurs	Andrew	30			--	Down	1803	Patty	Newry
Hutcheson	Robert	22			Lislane	Derry	1833-34	--	Derry
Hutchinson	William	--	Ann Jane	--	Coleraine	Derry	1847	Superior	Derry
Hutchison	John	--	Mary	--	Coleraine	Derry	1849	Garland	Derry
Inch	Chary	--			Faughanvale	Derry	1847	Barbara	Derry
Innes	Alexander	--			L'Derry	Derry	1850	Envoy	Derry
Irvin	John	--	Ellen	--	Ramelton	Donegal	1847	Venice	Derry
Irvine	Andrew	--			--	--	1811	Harmony	Derry
Irvine	John	--			--	--	1811	Harmony	Derry
Irwin	Catherine	--			Dunfanaghy	Donegal	1847	Barbara	Derry
Irwin	Isabella	--	Rebecca	--	Gallagh	Antrim	1849	Garland	Derry
Irwin	John	--			L'Derry	Derry	1850	Superior	Derry
Irwin	Nancy Jane	--			Dungiven	Derry	1848	HannahKerr	Derry
Irwin	William	--	Nancy	--	Ballymoney	Antrim	1849	Garland	Derry

Last Name	First Name	Age	Family	Age	Address	County	Date	Ship	Port
Jackson	William	--			L'Derry	Derry	1850	Superior	Derry
James	Margaret	--			N'tncunningham	Donegal	1850	Lumley	Derry
Jamison	Jane	19			Aghadowey	Derry	1834	--	Derry
Jamison	Sarah	--	MaryAnn	--	Moville	Donegal	1847	Hartford	Derry
Jamison	William	--			Coleraine	Derry	1850	Lumley	Derry
Jelly	Hugh	35			Loughinisland	Down	1804	Commerce	--
Jenars	Eliza	--			Omagh	Tyrone	1848	HannahKerr	Derry
Jervis	James	--			L'Derry	Derry	1847	Venice	Derry
Johnson	John	19			Connor	Antrim	1803	George	Belfast
Johnston	Eliza Jane	--			SixMileCross	Tyrone	1849	Envoy	Derry
Johnston	Ellan	--			Ballymoney	Antrim	1849	Garland	Derry
Johnston	John	18			Termaquin	Derry	1833-34	--	Derry
Johnston	John	23			Cumber	Derry	1803	Brutus	Derry
Johnston	Mary	--			Omagh	Tyrone	1848	HannahKerr	Derry
Johnston	Robert	--			Castledawson	Derry	1847	Montpellier	Derry
Johnston	Robert	15			Lochris	Donegal	1804	Catherine	Bally-shannon
Johnston	Samuel	--	Robert	--	Millford	Donegal	1848	HannahKerr	Derry
Johnston	William	--	Nancy	--	Castledawson	Derry	1847	Montpellier	Derry
			James	--					
			George	--					
			Rachel	8					
Johnston	William	12	Eliza	10	Ardstraw	Tyrone	1849	Garland	Derry
Jones	John	--			Raphoe	Donegal	1849	Envoy	Derry
Jones	Martha	--			Castleforward	Donegal	1847	Superior	Derry
Jones	Richard	24			Strabane	Tyrone	1803	Mohawk	Derry
Jordan	Rebecca	--			Taghboyne	Westmeath	1849	Envoy	Derry
Kane	Catherine	--			Limavady	Derry	1847	Allegheny	Derry
Kane	Catherine	--			N'tnstewart	Tyrone	1849	Superior	Derry
Kane	John	--			Ballynagard	Derry	1847	Hershell	Derry
Kane	John	--	Nancy	8	Garvagh	Derry	1849	Envoy	Derry
			Arthur	7					
Kane	Margaret	--			Ballynagard	Derry	1847	Hershell	Derry
Kane	Mary	--			Strabane	Tyrone	1848	HannahKerr	Derry

Last Name	First Name	Age	Family	Age	Address	County	Date	Ship	Port
Kane	Patrick	--			Limavady	Derry	1847	Venice	Derry
Kane	Sally	--			Draperstown	Derry	1847	Superior	Derry
Karlin	Patt	42			--	--	1804	Maria	Derry
Kavanagh	James	--			--	--	1811	Harmony	Derry
Kee	Charles	--	Eliza	--	Ballybofey	Donegal	1847	Barbara	Derry
			John	--					
			Mary	--					
			Thomas	3					
			George	1					
Keeland	Charles	--			Ramelton	Donegal	1847	Venice	Derry
Keenan	John	--	Patrick	8	Gortin	(*)	1849	Garland	Derry
			Mary	6					
Keenan	Mary	--			Gortin	(*)	1850	Superior	Derry
Keenon	Francis	--			Letterkenny	Donegal	1847	Hartford	Derry
Kelley	Michael	25			Omagh	Tyrone	1803	Brutus	Derry
Kelly	Ann	--			Ballybofey	Donegal	1847	Venice	Derry
Kelly	Arthur	--			Omagh	Tyrone	1847	Venice	Derry
Kelly	Catherine	--	Neal	--	Moville	Donegal	1847	Hershell	Derry
			Dennis	--					
			Catherine	--					
Kelly	Charles	21	Hugh	22	Dunmore	Tyrone	1804	Brothers	Derry
Kelly	Daniel	--			Ballynascreen	?	1849	Garland	Derry
Kelly	Dennis	--	Patrick	14	Castlefin	Donegal	1847	Allegheny	Derry
			Charles	12					
			Dennis	9					
			Francis	7					
			Mary	2					
Kelly	Edward	--	Patrick	--	Templemoyle	(*)	1847	Allegheny	Derry
			Edward	--					
			Magy	--					
Kelly	Elleanor	--	MaryAnn	--	Dungiven	Derry	1847	Allegheny	Derry

(*) See Endnotes

41

ULSTER EMIGRANTS TO PHILADELPHIA

Last Name	First Name	Age	Family	Age	Address	County	Date	Ship	Port
Kelly	Francis	--	Ann	--	Castlefin	Donegal	1847	Allegheny	Derry
			Patrick	--					
			Catherine	11					
			Bernard	8					
			Francis	6					
			Charles	2					
			Ann	6m					
Kelly	Hugh	30			Ballyshannon	Donegal	1804	Brothers	Derry
Kelly	James	--			Clougheneely	Donegal	1847	Venice	Derry
Kelly	James	--	Hugh	--	Carrygalt	Donegal	1847	Barbara	Derry
Kelly	James	--	James	12	Letterkenny	Donegal	1850	Lumley	Derry
			Mary	11					
Kelly	John	--			Draperstown	Derry	1847	Superior	Derry
Kelly	Margaret	--			Ramelton	Donegal	1847	Venice	Derry
Kelly	Mary	--			Beragh	Tyrone	1847	Venice	Derry
Kelly	Rose	--	Joseph	7	Ballybofey	Donegal	1848	HannahKerr	Derry
Kelly	Susan	--			Faughanvale	Derry	1847	Allegheny	Derry
Kelly	Susan	--	John	--	Castlefin	Donegal	1847	Hartford	Derry
Kelly	Thomas	36			Grange	Down	1803	George	Belfast
Kelly	William	20			Ballyscullion	Derry	1833-34	--	Derry
Kelly	William	23			Buncrana	Donegal	1803	Mohawk	Derry
Kenedy	John	41			--	Down	1803	Patty	Newry
Kennan	Thomas	25			Stewartstown	Tyrone	1803	Brutus	Derry
Kennedy	Alexander	--	Margaret	--	Coleraine	Derry	1849	Superior	Derry
			James	--					
Kennedy	Joseph	30	Jane	28	Ballywillin	Derry	1833-34	--	Derry
			Mary	7					
			Geroge	5					
			Fullerton	3					
			Infant (M)	1					
			Rachel	50					
Kennedy	Patt	52	Susan	52	Meenhallu	Donegal	1804	Catherine	Bally-shannon
			Edward	24					

Last Name	First Name	Age	Family	Age	Address	County	Date	Ship	Port
(Cont'd.)			John	19					
			James	13					
			Patrick	16					
			Charles	11					
Kennedy	Samuel	--			Coleraine	Derry	1850	Envoy	Derry
Keon	Margaret	--	Mary	--	Kesh	Fermanagh	1849	Garland	Derry
			Sarah	2					
Kerr	Allen	--			--	--	1811	Harmony	Derry
Kerr	Ann	--			Claudy	Derry	1847	Barbara	Derry
Kerr	Ann	--			Elagh	Tyrone	1849	Superior	Derry
Kerr	Charles	--			Ramelton	Donegal	1848	MaryCampbell	Derry
Kerr	Cornilius	--	Fanny	--	Dunfanaghy	Donegal	1847	Superior	Derry
			Ann	12					
			William	9					
			Catherine	7					
			Charles	5					
			Julian	3					
			James	1					
Kerr	David	--	Margaret	--	Waterside	Derry	1847	Barbara	Derry
			Margaret	--					
			Martha	--					
Kerr	Dennis	--	John	--	Rosnakill	Donegal	1847	MaryStewart	Derry
Kerr	Francis	--			Ramelton	Donegal	1848	MaryCampbell	Derry
Kerr	Jane	--			Cookstown	Tyrone	1847	Hartford	Derry
Kerr	John	--			--	--	1811	Fame	Derry
Kerr	John	22			Tam.Finlagan	Derry	1833-34	--	Derry
Kerr	Mary Ann	--	Catherine	10	Ballyboe	Donegal	1849	Envoy	Derry
			James	8					
Kerr	Matthew	--			--	--	1811	Fame	Derry
Kerrigan	Matilda	--			N'tnstewart	Tyrone	1847	Montpellier	Derry
Key	WIlliam	--			--	--	1811	Mary	Derry
Keys	Isabella	--			Kesh	Fermanagh	1850	Envoy	Derry
Kilday	Patrick	--			Churchill	Donegal	1849	Superior	Derry

ULSTER EMIGRANTS TO PHILADELPHIA

Last Name	First Name	Age	Family	Age	Address	County	Date	Ship	Port
Kilpatrick	James	--			Stranorlar	Donegal	1848	HannahKerr	Derry
Kilpatrick	Thomas	37			Killeaton	Antrim	1804	Commerce	--
Kilty	Joseph	--			L'Derry	Derry	1850	Envoy	Derry
Kincade	Matilda	--			St.Johnston	Donegal	1849	Superior	Derry
Kincaid	William	--	Eleanor	--	Raphoe	Donegal	1850	Superior	Derry
			Alexander	--					
			ElizaMary	--					
			Margaret	13					
			Alicia	10					
King	David	29			Cumber	Derry	1803	Brutus	Derry
King	James	45			Dungiven	Derry	1803	Penna.	Derry
King	Jane	--	Stewart	8	Dunnamanagh	Derry	1849	Garland	Derry
			Margaret	6					
			Thomas	3					
			Matilda	9m					
King	Robert	--			Letterkenny	Donegal	1850	Envoy	Derry
Kinney	Ellen	--			Dunnamanagh	Derry	1850	Superior	Derry
Kirgan	Ann	--			Cookstown	Tyrone	1847	Hartford	Derry
Kirk	Thomas	--			Glenmore	(*)	1847	Allegheny	Derry
Kirkman	James	40			--	--	1803	Edward	Belfast
Kirkpatrick	John	--			--	--	1811	Harmony	Derry
Kirkpatrick	William	--			--	--	1811	Harmony	Derry
Kirkwood	William	--	Rosanna	--	Leck	(*)	1847	Superior	Derry
			Sarah	10					
			Robert	6					
			William	3					
			James	6m					
Knox	Mary Jane	--			Culdaff	Donegal	1848	HannahKerr	Derry
Knox	William	--			L'Derry	Derry	1847	Venice	Derry
Knox	William	--			--	--	1811	Harmony	Derry
Kyle	Rosanna	--	Jane	--	Beragh	Tyrone	1847	Hartford	Derry

(*) See Endnotes

44

ULSTER EMIGRANTS TO PHILADELPHIA

Last Name	First Name	Age	Family	Age	Address	County	Date	Ship	Port
(Cont'd.)			Margaret	--					
			Catherine	--					
Labody	Robert	32			--	--	1803	Edward	Belfast
Lafferty	Biddy	--			Carne	Donegal	1849	Envoy	Derry
Lafferty	Daniel	--			Culdaff	Donegal	1848	HannahKerr	Derry
Lafferty	Elleanor	--			Glentogher	Donegal	1849	Envoy	Derry
Lafferty	John	--			Draperstown	Derry	1847	Venice	Derry
Laffety	James	--			Ramelton	Donegal	1847	Venice	Derry
Lagan	William	22			Burnally	Derry	1833-34	--	Derry
Lahey	Daniel	--			Stranorlar	Donegal	1849	Envoy	Derry
Lamon	Andrew	18			Ardegat	Donegal	1804	Catherine	Bally-shannon
Lane	Hugh	23			Clagan	Derry	1833-34	--	Derry
Langan	Bryan	--			Letterkenny	Donegal	1850	Envoy	Derry
Larkey	Michael	--			Moville	Donegal	1850	Superior	Derry
Larkie	Alexander	--	Mary	--	--	--	1811	Mary	Derry
Laverty	Elizabeth	20			--	--	1803	Active	Newry
Laverty	James	--			--	--	1811	Mary	Derry
Leaden	Patrick	--			Draperstown	Derry	1850	Superior	Derry
Lealer	Patrick	50			Strabane	Tyrone	1803	Penna.	Derry
Lecock	Joseph	--	MaryJane	--	Portstewart	Derry	1850	Superior	Derry
' Lee	Ephriam	26	Edward	23	Killashandra	Cavan	1803	George	Belfast
Leonard	John	--			Caven	Donegal	1847	Barbara	Derry
Leonard	Robert	21			--	--	1804	Maria	Derry
Lestly	George	30			Beatwell	Derry	1833	--	Derry
Lewis	Andrew	20			Limavady	Derry	1803	Penna.	Derry
Lewis	Fanny	70			Limavady	Derry	1803	Penna.	Derry
			Fanny, Jr.	15					
			George	33					
			John	33					
			Susan	36					
Liddle	Eliza Jane	--			Raphoe	Donegal	1850	Envoy	Derry

Last Name	First Name	Age	Family	Age	Address	County	Date	Ship	Port
Lindsay	William	--			Moville	Donegal	1850	Superior	Derry
Lindsey	Joseph	33			Sea Patrick	Down	1804	Commerce	--
Linsey	Sarah	20	Eliz.	18	Derrymore	Derry	1833-34	--	Derry
			James	20					
Linton	John	--	Mary	--	Coleraine	Derry	1847	Venice	Derry
Lithgow	William	--			Waterside	Derry	1847	Barbara	Derry
Little	John	25			Ballindrait	Donegal	1803	Penna.	Derry
Little	Robert	26			Ballindrait	Donegal	1803	Penna.	Derry
Little	Thomas	--	Samuel	--	Letterkenny	Donegal	1847	Venice	Derry
			Elizabeth	11					
Logan	George	25			Killinchy	Down	1804	Commerce	--
Logan	Mary	--			--	--	1811	Harmony	Derry
Logan	Thomas	--	Rebecca	--	Ramelton	Donegal	1849	Garland	Derry
Logue	Ellen	--	MaryJane	--	Muff	Derry	1849	Superior	Derry
Logue	James	--			--	--	1811	Harmony	Derry
Logue	James	--			Ragargam?	?	1848	MaryCampbell	Derry
Logue	John	18	Bernard	15	Killoyle	Derry	1833-34	--	Derry
Logue	Robert	--			Beragh	Tyrone	1848	MaryCampbell	Derry
Logue	William	--	John	--	Beragh	Tyrone	1849	Envoy	Derry
Logue	William	--			--	--	1811	Harmony	Derry
Logue	William	--			Moville	Donegal	1849	Envoy	Derry
Long	Fanny	--			Castlefin	Donegal	1848	HannahKerr	Derry
Long	William	--			Limavady	Derry	1849	Superior	Derry
Longe	Michael	--	Fanny	--	Rosnakill	Donegal	1847	MaryStewart	Derry
			James	13					
			Mary	10					
			Patrick	8					
			Grace	5					
			Nelly	3					
			Nancy	1					
Longe	Neal	--	Paddy	--	Rosnakill	Donegal	1847	MaryStewart	Derry
			Grace	--					
			Neal	--					

Last Name	First Name	Age	Family	Age	Address	County	Date	Ship	Port
(Cont'd.)			Thomas	--					
Looney	Christopher	--	Catherine	--	Omagh	Tyrone	1849	Superior	Derry
			Christopher	9					
			Hugh	7					
			Michael	5					
			John	3					
Loughead	Edward	--	Catherine	--	--	--	1811	Harmony	Derry
Loughery	James	--	Margaret	--	Lifford	(*)	1849	Envoy	Derry
Loughrey	Eliza	--	Jane	--	Balteagh	(*)	1849	Envoy	Derry
Loughridge	William	30	Mg.	24	Cookstown	Tyrone	1803	Strafford	Derry
			Jane	7					
			Elizabeth	2					
			James	5					
Loughry	Louisa	--	MaryAnn	--	Limavady	Derry	1847	Venice	Derry
Lowden	James	40	Jane	36	Bovevagh	Derry	1833-34	--	Derry
			Mary	3					
			John	1					
Lowry	Arthur	--	Elizabeth	--	--	--	1847	Superior	Derry
			Isabella	12					
Lowry	James	--	Jane	--	N'tncunningham	Donegal	1847	Superior	Derry
Lowry	John	32	Mary	30	Magheramore	Derry	1833-34	--	Derry
Lowry	Robert	--			N'tncunningham	Donegal	1850	Lumley	Derry
Lowry	William	29			Killinchy	Down	1803	George	Belfast
Lucas	Adam	--			Strabane	Tyrone	1849	Superior	Derry
Lungan	Catherine	--	Ann	--	Killygordon	(*)	1847	MaryStewart	Derry
Lunny	Pat	20			Enniskillen	Fermanagh	1803	Mohawk	Derry
Lurkie	Jane	--			--	--	1811	Mary	Derry
Luss	Susanna	--			Coleraine	Derry	1849	Superior	Derry
Lynagh	Patrick	--	Michael	--	Carrygalt	Donegal	1847	Hershell	Derry
			Sophia	--					
			Patrick	--					
Lynch	Ann	--			Beragh	Tyrone	1849	Envoy	Derry

(*) See Endnotes

ULSTER EMIGRANTS TO PHILADELPHIA

Last Name	First Name	Age	Family	Age	Address	County	Date	Ship	Port
Lynch	Catherine	--			Waterside	Derry	1847	Venice	Derry
Lynch	Catherine	--	John	--	Letterkenny	Donegal	1847	Venice	Derry
			Hugh	--					
			Ann	11					
			Ellen	6					
			Sarah	2					
Lynch	Charles	--			Feeny	Derry	1847	Superior	Derry
Lynch	Christopher	--			Ramelton	Donegal	1850	Envoy	Derry
Lynch	Elizabeth	--	John	--	Ballybofey	Donegal	1848	HannahKerr	Derry
Lynch	Elleanor	--			St.Johnston	Donegal	1849	Envoy	Derry
Lynch	Hannah	--			Ballyboe	Donegal	1849	Envoy	Derry
Lynch	James	--			Limavady	Derry	1847	Hartford	Derry
Lynch	John	--			Dunnamanagh	Derry	1847	Barbara	Derry
Lynch	Joseph	--	Sally	--	Omagh	Tyrone	1850	Superior	Derry
Lynch	Mary	--			Moville	Donegal	1850	Envoy	Derry
Lynch	Nancy	--			Burnfoot	Donegal	1849	Superior	Derry
Lynch	Patrick	27			--	Tyrone	1803	Patty	Newry
Lynch	Richard	--			Culdaff	Donegal	1848	HannahKerr	Derry
Lynchakin	Denis	20			Buncrana	Donegal	1803	Mohawk	Derry
Lynn	Edward	--			Coleraine	Derry	1847	Allegheny	Derry
Lynn	Mary Jane	--	Jane	9	Coleraine	Derry	1849	Superior	Derry
Lynn	Samuel	--			Coleraine	Derry	1849	Garland	Derry
Lyons	Oliver	--			Coleraine	Derry	1849	Superior	Derry
Lytle	Joseph	--	Sarah	--	Donegal	Donegal	1850	Envoy	Derry
			Margaret	--					
			Mary	--					
			Joseph	11					
			Esther	7					
Macky	Robert	--	Sarah	--	Coleraine	Derry	1849	Envoy	Derry
Magee	Mary	--			Ballybofey	Donegal	1848	HannahKerr	Derry
Magis	Joseph	--			--	--	1811	Mary	Derry
Maguire	Bridget	36			Lurgan	(*)	1804	Jefferson	Bally-shannon

(*) See Endnotes

Last Name	First Name	Age	Family	Age	Address	County	Date	Ship	Port
Maguire	Catherine	--	Charles	8	Ballybofey	Donegal	1848	HannahKerr	Derry
			Francis	6					
			John	3					
			Hugh	1					
Maguire	Francis	38			Lurgan	(*)	1804	Jefferson	Bally-shannon
Maguire	James	--	William	--	Cookstown	Tyrone	1850	Superior	Derry
			Ann	--					
			Margaret	--					
Maguire	Sarah	--	James	--	N'tnstewart	Tyrone	1849	Superior	Derry
			Mary	11					
			Jane	9					
			Patrick	7					
			Bernard	5					
			Sarah	9m					
			Dennis	7					
Mairs	Ann	43	Margaret	18	Ballylough	Derry	1834	--	Derry
			Sarah	13					
			Jane	10					
			Matilda	3					
Mairs	Soba	40			Ballylough	Derry	1834	--	Derry
Malin	Patrick	--	Patrick	--	Ardmalin	Donegal	1847	Hartford	Derry
			Daniel	12					
			Bridget	8					
Marlow	Owen	--			Ballygawley	(*)	1849	Envoy	Derry
Martin	Anne	20			Enniskillen	Fermanagh	1803	Mohawk	Derry
Martin	Daniel	22			Ardnargle	Derry	1833-34	--	Derry
Martin	George	35			Blaris	Down	1804	Commerce	--
Martin	James	--			--	--	1811	Fame	Derry
Martin	John	21			--	--	1803	Edward	Belfast
Martin	Martha	--			--	--	1811	Fame	Derry
Martin	Sameul	--			--	--	1811	Fame	Derry

(*) See Endnotes

ULSTER EMIGRANTS TO PHILADELPHIA

Last Name	First Name	Age	Family	Age	Address	County	Date	Ship	Port
Martine	William	--	Margaret	--	Aghadowey	Derry	1849	Envoy	Derry
Mathews	Thomas	27	Elizabeth	25	Belfast	Antrim	1803	George	Belfast
Matson	Eliza	--			Millford	Donegal	1847	Barbara	Derry
Maugher	Edward	26			--	Queens	1803	Patty	Newry
Maxwell	George	24			Raferty	Donegal	1804	Catherine	Bally-shannon
Maxwell	Nancy	30	Robert	10	Clanely	Tyrone	1803	Penna.	Derry
Maze	Francis	--			--	--	1811	Mary	Derry
McAdoo	Eliza	--	Elizabeth	--	St.Johnston	Donegal	1850	Superior	Derry
			Robert	--					
			Elizabeth	--					
McAfee	Agnes	20			Belfast	Antrim	1804	Commerce	--
McAfee	Jane	--			Bushmills	Antrim	1847	Hershell	Derry
McAfee	Samuel	--			Coleraine	Derry	1847	Superior	Derry
McAlary	Lusinda	--			St.Johnston	Donegal	1849	Envoy	Derry
McAleer	John	--			Gortin	(*)	1849	Garland	Derry
McAleer	Mary	--			Gortin	(*)	1849	Envoy	Derry
McAleer	Michael	--			Carrigalt	Donegal	1848	HannahKerr	Derry
McAlister	Margaret	--	WIlliam	--	Bridge End	Donegal	1850	Superior	Derry
			Biddy	--					
McAlister	William	--	Nancy	--	Ballybofey	Donegal	1848	HannahKerr	Derry
			Elizabeth	--					
McAllister	Hugh	26			Boghill	Derry	1833-34	--	Derry
McAllister	William	--	William	--	Creeslough	Donegal	1847	MaryStewart	Derry
			Sarah Jane	--					
McAna	Barry	24			Strabane	Tyrone	1803	Mohawk	Derry
McAnaspie	James	--			Ballygawley	(*)	1849	Garland	Derry
McAneny	Margaret	--	James	--	N'tnstewart	Tyrone	1849	Garland	Derry
			Margaret	--					
			Catherine	10					
			Peter	8					
McAneny	Thomas	--	Sarah	--	Omagh	Tyrone	1848	HannahKerr	Derry

(*) See Endnotes

Last Name	First Name	Age	Family	Age	Address	County	Date	Ship	Port
(Cont'd.)			Rosey	--					
McAnespy	John	--			Ballygawley	(*)	1850	Envoy	Derry
McAnulty	George	--	Biddy	--	L'Derry	Derry	1847	Montpellier	Derry
			Edward	10					
			Catherine	7					
			George	4					
McAnulty	Margaret	--			Letterkenny	Donegal	1850	Envoy	Derry
McAnulty	William	--			Creeslough	Donegal	1847	MaryStewart	Derry
McArthur	Robert	--	John	--	--	--	1811	Fame	Derry
- McAshee	Francis	--	Thomas	--	Strabane	Tyrone	1847	Montpellier	Derry
McAteer	Michael	--			Fanad	Donegal	1847	Superior	Derry
McAvay	Margaret	--	John	--	Raphoe	Donegal	1849	Superior	Derry
McAward	Ferrol	21			Buncrana	Donegal	1803	Mohawk	Derry
McAwly	Alexander	--			Dunfanaghy	Donegal	1850	Envoy	Derry
McBriarty	James	--	Bridget	--	Glenmore	(*)	1847	Allegheny	Derry
			Francis	3					
			Rose Ann	1					
McBriarty	Patrick	--			Clougheneely	Donegal	1847	Venice	Derry
McBride	Betty	--			Carrygalt	Donegal	1847	Barbara	Derry
McBride	Catherine	--			Millford	Donegal	1847	Superior	Derry
McBride	Hugh	26	William	25	--	--	1803	Edward	Belfast
McBride	Mary	--			Ballybofey	Donegal	1849	Envoy	Derry
McBride	Neal	--	Anne	--	Ballybofey	Donegal	1849	Envoy	Derry
			Biddy	11					
McBride	Samuel	28			--	Tyrone	1803	Patty	Newry
McBride	William	50			Dungiven	Derry	1803	Penna.	Derry
McBrine	Jane	--			--	--	1811	Mary	Derry
McBrine	Patrick	--			N'tnstewart	Tyrone	1847	Superior	Derry
McCad	John	29			Bushmills	Antrim	1803	Brutus	Derry
McCafferty	Bernard	--			Ballybofey	Donegal	1848	HannahKerr	Derry
McCafferty	Biddy	20			Meenhallu	Donegal	1804	Catherine	Bally-shannon

(*) See Endnotes

ULSTER EMIGRANTS TO PHILADELPHIA

Last Name	First Name	Age	Family	Age	Address	County	Date	Ship	Port
McCafferty	Edward	--			--	--	1811	Harmony	Derry
McCafferty	John	--	Elizabeth	--	Ramelton	Donegal	1847	Montpellier	Derry
			Catherine	--					
McCaffry	Biddy	--			Kesh	Fermanagh	1850	Superior	Derry
McCaffry	Teragh	--			Beragh	Tyrone	1849	Superior	Derry
McCahill	Conoly	--	Dennis	--	Raphoe	Donegal	1849	Superior	Derry
			Magy	--					
McCalister	Keatty	--			Maghera	Donegal	1849	Garland	Derry
McCall	Eliza	--			Limavady	Derry	1850	Envoy	Derry
McCallen	Patrick	33			Tullaghan	Donegal	1803	Penna.	Derry
McCallion	Mary	--			L'Derry	Derry	1847	Venice	Derry
McCandless	Hugh	--	Eliz. Ann	--	Coleraine	Derry	1849	Superior	Derry
McCanlis	John	25			Ballymore	Derry	1833-34	--	Derry
McCann	Fanny	--			Buncrana	Donegal	1847	Venice	Derry
McCann	James	--			Ballynascreen	?	1849	Garland	Derry
McCann	Margaret	--			L'Derry	Derry	1849	Superior	Derry
McCann	Michael	--	Mary	--	Moville	Donegal	1847	Hershell	Derry
McCann	Rose	--			Maghera	Donegal	1850	Envoy	Derry
McCanna	Barny	43			--	--	1804	Maria	Derry
McCanny	John	--	Nathaniel	--	Ballybofey	Donegal	1848	HannahKerr	Derry
McCanny	Margaret	--	Francis	9	Strabane	Tyrone	1847	Montpellier	Derry
McCanny	Nancy	--			Drumquin	Tyrone	1850	Envoy	Derry
McCaraher	Eliza	--	Sarah	12	Armoy	Antrim	1847	Superior	Derry
			Neil	9					
McCarney	Patrick	--	Bridget	--	Fintona	Tyrone	1850	Envoy	Derry
McCarroll	Patrick	26			Augher	Tyrone	1804	Commerce	---
McCarroll	Susanna	--			Ballymoney	Antrim	1847	Venice	Derry
McCarron	William	--			Coleraine	Derry	1849	Garland	Derry
McCarter	Daniel	--	Thomas	--	Ballycastle	Derry	1850	Superior	Derry
McCash	John	60	Jane	56	Largy	Derry	1833-34	--	Derry
			William	30					
			Joseph	24					
			Hugh	22					

ULSTER EMIGRANTS TO PHILADELPHIA

Last Name	First Name	Age	Family	Age	Address	County	Date	Ship	Port
McCaughty	Robert	25	Jane	20	Carmoney	Antrim	1804	Commerce	--
McCauley	John	--			Ballymoney	Antrim	1850	Superior	Derry
McCauley	Robert	30			Ballyleighery	Derry	1833-34	--	Derry
McCausland	James	--			St.Johnston	Donegal	1849	Envoy	Derry
McCausland	John	--			Beragh	Tyrone	1847	Superior	Derry
McCausland	John	--	MaryEiza	--	St.Johnston	Donegal	1849	Envoy	Derry
			James	9m					
McCay	Annie	--			Strabane	Tyrone	1848	HannahKerr	Derry
McCay	Eliza	11	Prudence	6	Maghera	Donegal	1849	Garland	Derry
McCay	Hugh	--			Clonmany	Donegal	1847	Superior	Derry
McCay	Mary	--			Clonmany	Donegal	1847	Superior	Derry
McCay	Rosey	--			Glenmore	(*)	1847	Allegheny	Derry
McClafferty	Bryan	--	Rosey	--	Cross Roads	Donegal	1847	Hershell	Derry
McClafferty	Isabella	--			Cross Roads	Donegal	1847	Hershell	Derry
McClafferty	William	--			Millford	Donegal	1848	MaryCampbell	Derry
McClain	James	--			Dunfanaghy	Donegal	1848	MaryCampbell	Derry
McClaren	Edward	--			Faughanvale	Derry	1848	MaryCampbell	Derry
McClay	Allen	--			Ards	Donegal	1849	Envoy	Derry
McClay	Arthur	--	Margaret	--	Castlemellan	Tyrone	1849	Envoy	Derry
McClay	Eliz	--			Letterkenny	Donegal	1850	Superior	Derry
McClay	Elleanor	--	Daniel	--	Ballybegly	Donegal	1847	Allegheny	Derry
			Patrick	--					
			Margaret	--					
			Philip	--					
McClean	Archibold	--	Mary Jane	--	Ballykelly	Derry	1847	Hartford	Derry
			Martha	3					
			Robert	3m					
McClean	Margaret	--			Millford	Donegal	1847	Superior	Derry
McClelland	James	--	William	--	Coleraine	Derry	1849	Superior	Derry
			Margaret	--					
			John	--					
			Eliz. Ann	--					

(*) See Endnotes

ULSTER EMIGRANTS TO PHILADELPHIA

Last Name	First Name	Age	Family	Age	Address	County	Date	Ship	Port
(Cont'd.)			Robert	--					
			Cochran	--					
			Thomas	--					
McClelland	Margaret	--			Dungiven	Derry	1848	MaryCampbell	Derry
McClelland	Margaret	--	Ross	10	Strabane	Tyrone	1847	Barbara	Derry
McClelland	Mary	--	Biddy	--	Coleraine	Derry	1848	HannahKerr	Derry
McClelland	Thomas	--			Coleraine	Derry	1849	Garland	Derry
McClelland	William	--	Margaret	--	Coleraine	Derry	1849	Superior	Derry
			Martha	--					
			Joseph	--					
			Nancy	--					
McClenahan	Margaret	--	Eliza	11	Coleraine	Derry	1849	Garland	Derry
			Margaret	8					
			Nancy	6					
			Hugh	2					
			Margaret	--					
McClintock	Eliza	--	Sarah	--	Castlefin	Donegal	1850	Superior	Derry
			John	2					
			William	6m					
McClintock	James	--	Mary	--	Whitehouse	Donegal	1847	Barbara	Derry
			Susanna	--					
			John	--					
			Rebecca	--					
			Mary	11					
			Elizabeth	9					
McClintock	Margaret	--			Raphoe	Donegal	1849	Superior	Derry
McClintock	Rebecca	--			Omagh	Tyrone	1849	Envoy	Derry
McClintock	William	--	Jane	--	Omagh	Tyrone	1849	Envoy	Derry
			James	11					
			William	3					
			Robert	2					
			Margaret	3m					

ULSTER EMIGRANTS TO PHILADELPHIA

Last Name	First Name	Age	Family	Age	Address	County	Date	Ship	Port
McCloskey	Bryan	--	Ellen	--	Draperstown	Derry	1847	Superior	Derry
			Michael	6m					
			James	--					
			Rose	--					
McCloskey	James	--			--	--	1811	Fame	Derry
McCloskey	James	26	Jane	28	Bolea	Derry	1833-34	--	Derry
McCloskey	John	--			Feeny	Derry	1847	Superior	Derry
McCloskey	Patrick	--			Feeny	Derry	1847	Superior	Derry
McCloskey	Sarah	--			Dungiven	Derry	1848	HannahKerr	Derry
McCloskey	William	--			Dungiven	Derry	1848	HannahKerr	Derry
McClosky	Isabella	--	Owen	2	Ballykelly	Derry	1847	Allegheny	Derry
McClosky	John	25	Rose	19	Drimreny	Donegal	1804	Catherine	Bally-shannon
McClosky	Mary	--	Rose	--	Garvagh	Derry	1847	Venice	Derry
McClure	David	12			Castlederg	Tyrone	1850	Envoy	Derry
McCoach	Mary	--	Ellen	--	Tamney	Donegal	1847	Barbara	Derry
McColgan	James	--	Sally	--	Ballygorman	Donegal	1847	Barbara	Derry
McColgan	Mary Ann	--	Peggy	--	Carne	Donegal	1849	Envoy	Derry
McColgan	Willian	--			L'Derry	Derry	1850	Superior	Derry
McColley	Alicia Ann	--	Thomas	11	N'tncunningham	Donegal	1849	Superior	Derry
McCollum	Margaret	--	Martha	--	Letterkenny	Donegal	1849	Envoy	Derry
McConaghy	David	30			Ballyartan	Derry	1803	Mohawk	Derry
McConnell	James	--			--	--	1811	Fame	Derry
McConnell	John	--	Mary	--	Ballymoney	Antrim	1850	Superior	Derry
			Mary Ann	--					
			Sarah	5					
			Nancy	1					
McConnell	Margaret	--			L'Derry	Derry	1850	Envoy	Derry
McConnell	Rebecca	--	Mary	--	Enniskillen	Fermanagh	1849	Superior	Derry
			Mary Ann	11					
			John	7					
			Thomas	5					
			Jane	2					

ULSTER EMIGRANTS TO PHILADELPHIA

Last Name	First Name	Age	Family	Age	Address	County	Date	Ship	Port
McConnell	Mary	--			Letterkenny	Donegal	1849	Envoy	Derry
McConnell	William	--	Jane	--	Church Hill	Donegal	1848	HannahKerr	Derry
			William	11					
			Marg.Jane	8					
			Eliza	4					
			John	5					
			Samuel	3m					
McConologhe	Unity	--			Clonmany	Donegal	1849	Envoy	Derry
McConologue	James	--	William	--	Churchill	Donegal	1849	Superior	Derry
McConomy	Daniel	--			Dunfanaghy	Donegal	1849	Envoy	Derry
McConomy	Magg	--	Keatty	--	Dunfanaghy	Derry	1850	Envoy	Derry
			Fanny	--					
			Daniel	--					
McConway	John	28	Mary	26	--	--	1804	Maria	Derry
McCook	James	22	John	20	Tam.Finlagan	Derry	1833-34	--	Derry
McCool	John	21			Terrydremont	Derry	1833-34	--	Derry
McCord	Margaret	--			Millford	Donegal	1847	Superior	Derry
McCormick	Daniel	--			Killygordon	(*)	1847	Superior	Derry
McCormick	Ellanor	--			Glenmore	(*)	1847	Allegheny	Derry
McCormick	John	--	Bernard	--	Limavady	Derry	1847	Venice	Derry
			Mary	12					
			Margaret	10					
			Biddy	7					
McCormick	Katty	--			Convoy	Donegal	1849	Superior	Derry
McCormick	Patrick	--	Sally	--	Limavady	Derry	1847	Venice	Derry
McCormick	Patrick	25	William	23		Duncrun	Derry	1833-34	--
McCotter	Wiliam	--			Ballymoney	Antrim	1850	Superior	Derry
McCoun	Charles	--			--	--	1811	Harmony	Derry
McCoy	James	--			Rosnakill	Donegal	1849	Superior	Derry
McCoy	John	20			Clogher	(*)	1803	Mohawk	Derry
McCracken	James	--	Mary	--	Cookstown	Tyrone	1847	Hartford	Derry
			Henry	--					
			Jane	3m					

(*) See Endnotes

ULSTER EMIGRANTS TO PHILADELPHIA

Last Name	First Name	Age	Family	Age	Address	County	Date	Ship	Port
McCracken	John	--			Balteagh	(*)	1849	Envoy	Derry
McCrea	?	--			Farmhill	(*)	1847	Montpellier	Derry
McCrea	James	--	William	--	Strabane	Tyrone	1847	Montpellier	Derry
McCrea	John	24			Drumhome	Donegal	1804	Catherine	Bally-shannon
McCrea	Robert	30			Strabane	Tyrone	1803	Mohawk	Derry
McCrorey	Miles	--			Castlederg	Tyrone	1847	Superior	Derry
McCrory	Biddy	--	Margaret	--	Bloomhill	Tyrone	1848	MaryCampbell	Derry
			Ann	9					
			Hugh	7					
			Bridget	5					
McCrory	Hugh	--	Hugh	--	Dunfanaghy	Donegal	1847	Barbara	Derry
McCrossan	Charles	--	William	--	N'tnstewart	Tyrone	1847	Montpellier	Derry
McCrossan	John	--			N'tnstewart	Tyrone	1849	Superior	Derry
McCue	Daniel	--			--	--	1811	Harmony	Derry
McCue	Hugh	--			Castlederg	Tyrone	1847	Montpellier	Derry
McCue	Michael	--			--	--	1811	Harmony	Derry
McCullagh	Alice	--			Omagh	Tyrone	1847	Barbara	Derry
McCullagh	Daniel	--			Gortin	(*)	1847	Montpellier	Derry
McCullagh	Jane	--			Prehen	Derry	1847	Venice	Derry
McCullagh	John	--	Mary	--	Draperstown	Derry	1850	Superior	Derry
			Catherine	12					
			Pat	7					
			William	5					
McCullagh	Sally	--	Rosy	--	Gortin	(*)	1847	Hartford	Derry
McCullough	Hers.	27			--	--	1803	Edward	Belfast
McCullough	James	--	Elizabeth	--	Coleraine	Derry	1849	Superior	Derry
McCully	Andrew	50	Catherine	48	Dirnaflaw	Derry	1833-34	--	Derry
McCurdy	Eliza	12	Jane	10	Coleraine	Derry	1849	Garland	Derry
McCurdy	Margaret	--			Coleraine	Derry	1847	Barbara	Derry
			Margaret	9					
			Nancy	8					

(*) See Endnotes

ULSTER EMIGRANTS TO PHILADELPHIA

Last Name	First Name	Age	Family	Age	Address	County	Date	Ship	Port
McCurdy	William	--	Morgan	--	--	--	1811	Mary	Derry
McCusker	Philip	--			Beragh	Tyrone	1849	Superior	Derry
*McCutcheon	George	--	Eliza	--	Omagh	Tyrone	1847	Hartford	Derry
			Marg.Jane	--					
			Martha	--					
			Mary	--					
			George	--					
McDade	Alice	--	Patrick	2	Letterkenny	Donegal	1850	Envoy	Derry
			Margaret	--					
McDade	Biddy	--			Fanad	Donegal	1847	Hershell	Derry
McDade	Charles	--			Burnfoot	Donegal	1849	Superior	Derry
McDade	Elleanor	--			Londonderry	Derry	1847	Hershell	Derry
McDade	Fanny	--	Mary	--	Castlederg	Tyrone	1848	MaryCampbell	Derry
McDade	James	--	Mary	--	Rathmullan	Donegal	1849	Garland	Derry
			Thomas	12					
McDade	James	22			Killarhel	Donegal	1804	Catherine	Bally-shannon
McDade	Mary Ann	--			Ramelton	Dongal	1847	Venice	Derry
McDade	Owen	28			Carne	Donegal	1803	Mohawk	Derry
McDade	Unity	--			Termon	Donegal	1850	Envoy	Derry
McDale	John	36			--	Down	1803	Patty	Newry
McDermott	Catherine	--	Ellen	10	Whitecastle	Donegal	1850	Envoy	Derry
			Ann	6					
McDermott	Edward	--	John	--	Carrakeel	(*)	1847	Venice	Derry
McDermott	Mary	--			Beragh	Tyrone	1849	Envoy	Derry
McDermott	Patrick	--			Beragh	Tyrone	1848	MaryCampbell	Derry
McDevitt	Catherine	--	Margaret	12	Claudy	Derry	1849	Superior	Derry
			Francis	4					
McDevitt	Neal	--			Ramelton	Donegal	1847	Hershell	Derry
McDivett	Columb	--			Letterkenny	Donegal	1847	Barbara	Derry
McDivett	Daniel	--	Jane	--	Ramelton	Donegal	1847	Hershell	Derry
			Mary	--					

(*) See Endnotes

ULSTER EMIGRANTS TO PHILADELPHIA

Last Name	First Name	Age	Family	Age	Address	County	Date	Ship	Port
McDivett	Francis	--			Ballybofey	Donegal	1848	HannahKerr	Derry
McDivett	Henry	--			Moville	Donegal	1850	Envoy	Derry
McDivett	Mary	--			Coleraine	Derry	1847	MaryStewart	Derry
McDivett	Peggy	--			Culdaff	Donegal	1848	HannahKerr	Derry
McDivett	William	--			Londonderry	Derry	1847	Hershell	Derry
McDivett	William	--			St.Johnston	Donegal	1848	HannahKerr	Derry
McDivitt	Susan	--			Aghadowey	Derry	1847	Venice	Derry
McDonald	Isabella	--	Matilda	--	Ballykelly	Derry	1848	MaryCampbell	Derry
McDonnell	Patrick	20			Buncrana	Donegal	1803	Mohawk	Derry
McDougall	John	--			Letterkenny	Donegal	1847	Venice	Derry
McElain	Margeret	--			Beragh	Tyrone	1849	Superior	Derry
McElhenny	Jane	--			Letterkenny	Donegal	1850	Lumley	Derry
McElhenny	Thomas	--			Dungiven	Derry	1848	MaryCampbell	Derry
McElhinny	Catherine	--			Waterside	Derry	1847	Venice	Derry
McEliney	James	--			Clonmany	Donegal	1847	Superior	Derry
McElroy	Ann	--	Isabella	--	Castlederg	Tyrone	1848	MaryCampbell	Derry
McElroy	George	--	& Family	--	--	--	1811	Fame	Derry
McElwee	Charles	--	Catherine	--	Ramelton	Donegal	1847	Allegheny	Derry
McEntyre	Robert	28			Collins	Derry	1833-34	--	Derry
McErlain	Catherine	--			Moville	Donegal	1850	Superior	Derry
McEvay	James	11	Ellen	9					
			Patrick	7					
			Andrew	5					
			Bridget	3					
			Ann	1					
McEvay	Sally	--	Barney	--	Convoy	Donegal	1850	Envoy	Derry
			Daniel	--					
			Hugh	--					
McFadden	Ann	--			Clougheneely	Donegal	1847	Venice	Derry
McFadden	Dominick	--			Dunfanaghy	Donegal	1847	Hershell	Derry
McFadden	John	--			Cranslough	Tyrone	1847	Hartford	Derry
McFadden	John	--			Crossroads	Donegal	1850	Envoy	Derry
McFadden	Mary	--			Rathmullan	Donegal	1849	Garland	Derry

ULSTER EMIGRANTS TO PHILADELPHIA

Last Name	First Name	Age	Family	Age	Address	County	Date	Ship	Port
McFadden	Neal	--	Uny	--	Carrygalt	Donegal	1847	Barbara	Derry
			Paddy	4					
McFaddin	Manus	--	Eleanor	--	--	--	1811	Harmony	Derry
McFarland	Andrew	--			Omagh	Tyrone	1847	Montpellier	Derry
McFarland	Isabella	--	Anne	13	SixMileCross	Tyrone	1849	Envoy	Derry
McFarland	John	--			Faughanvale	Derry	1847	Barbara	Derry
McFarland	John	--	Elizabeth	--	Beragh	Tyrone	1850	Superior	Derry
			James	--					
			Catherine	--					
			Jane	--					
			Eliza	11					
			Bill	9					
			William	6					
McFarland	John	--	Margaret	--	Omagh	Tyrone	1847	Hartford	Derry
McFarland	Joseph	--			Beragh	Tyrone	1849	Superior	Derry
McFarland	Samuel	--			Dunnamanagh	Derry	1849	Garland	Derry
McFauls	Margaret	--			Garvagh	Derry	1848	MaryCampbell	Derry
McFeeters	Eliza Jane	--			Letterkenny	Donegal	1850	Envoy	Derry
McFetrick	Jane	--	David	--	Ballybofey	Donegal	1848	Hannah Kerr	Derry
McFetridge	Isabella	--			Coleraine	Derry	1848	Hannah Kerr	Derry
McFetridge	John	24			Lands Agivey	Derry	1834	--	Derry
McFetridge	Joseph	--			Letterkenny	Donegal	1847	Barbara	Derry
McFetridge	Robert	18			Ballyriskmore	Derry	1833-34	--	Derry
McFetridge	William	22			Collins	Derry	1833-34	--	Derry
McGafferty	Pat	19			Taughblane	Down	1803	Mohawk	Derry
McGahey	Ellen M.	--			N'tnstewart	Tyrone	1850	Superior	Derry
McGan	John	34	Elizabeth	30	Coagh	Tyrone	1803	Strafford	Derry
			Sarah	2					
			Elinor	1					
McGarity	Mary	--			Ballybofey	Donegal	1848	Hannah Kerr	Derry
McGarity	Mary	--			Letterkenny	Donegal	1847	Hartford	Derry
McGarrity	Ellen	--	Sophia	--	N'tnstewart	Tyrone	1850	Lumley	Derry
McGarry	Mary	--			Buncrana	Donegal	1849	Envoy	Derry

ULSTER EMIGRANTS TO PHILADELPHIA

Last Name	First Name	Age	Family	Age	Address	County	Date	Ship	Port
McGarvey	Ellen	--			L'Derry	Derry	1849	Envoy	Derry
McGarvey	James	--			Creeslough	Donegal	1847	Mary Stewart	Derry
McGarvey	Susanna	--			N'tnstewart	Tyrone	1849	Superior	Derry
McGarvey	William	--	Elizabeth	--	Fanad	Donegal	1847	Superior	Derry
McGeady	Hugh	--	Fanny	--	Letterkenny	Donegal	1847	Superior	Derry
			William	10					
McGeeghan	James	--			L'Derry	Derry	1849	Superior	Derry
McGeighan	Dennis	--			L'Derry	Derry	1849	Superior	Derry
McGellaghan	Patrick	--			--	--	1811	Mary	Derry
McGeoghan	Mary	--			L'Derry	Derry	1847	Hershell	Derry
McGerrigan	Hugh	--			Millford	Donegal	1848	Hannah Kerr	Derry
McGettigan	Grace	--	Elleanor	--	Craigdoo	Donegal	1847	Montpellier	Derry
McGettigan	Robert	--			Raphoe	Donegal	1849	Superior	Derry
McGhee	Mary	--			Glenalla	Donegal	1847	Allegheny	Derry
McGheeghan	James	--			Letterkenny	Donegal	1847	Venice	Derry
McGinley	Cornelius	--			Ramelton	Donegal	1847	Hershell	Derry
McGinley	Grace	--			Dunfanaghy	Donegal	1847	Hershell	Derry
McGinley	James	--			Crossroads	Donegal	1847	Montpellier	Derry
McGinley	Mickey	--			Dunfanaghy	Donegal	1848	HannahKerr	Derry
McGinness	John	--			Culdaff	Donegal	1848	HannahKerr	Derry
McGinnis	John	--	Mary	--	Muff	Derry	1849	Garland	Derry
McGinty	Patrick	--	Anne	--	Donegal	Donegal	1849	Garland	Derry
			Charles	13					
			Patrick	11					
			James	9					
			Anne	7					
			John	4					
			Mary	6					
			Catherine	3m					
McGirk	John	--			Beragh	Tyrone	1847	Superior	Derry
McGlensay	Margaret	--			Churchill	Donegal	1847	Hartford	Derry
McGlone	John	--	James	--	Cookstown	Tyrone	1849	Superior	Derry
			Bridget	--					

ULSTER EMIGRANTS TO PHILADELPHIA

Last Name	First Name	Age	Family	Age	Address	County	Date	Ship	Port
McGloughlin	Owen	29	Nelly	30	Glen	Donegal	1804	Catherine	Bally-shannon
			a child	5					
McGlynn	John	--			Letterkenny	Donegal	1847	Venice	Derry
McGomery	Mary	17			--	--	1804	Maria	Derry
McGonagall	James	36			Tullaghan	Donegal	1803	Penna.	Derry
McGonegall	James	25			Buncrana	Donegal	1803	Mohawk	Derry
McGonegle	Bridget	--	Peggy	8	Straid	(*)	1850	Envoy	Derry
			Edward	4					
McGonegle	Charles	--			Omagh	Tyrone	1850	Superior	Derry
McGonigle	Daniel	--			Clonmany	Donegal	1849	Envoy	Derry
McGonigle	Dennis	--			Ballybofey	Donegal	1848	HannahKerr	Derry
McGonigle	Margaret	5	John	3	Lands Agivey	Derry	1834	--	Derry
McGorman	John	--			Burnfoot	Donegal	1850	Envoy	Derry
McGowan	Nancy	--			Raphoe	Donegal	1850	Superior	Derry
McGowan	Philip	--			--	--	1811	Harmony	Derry
McGowan	William	35			Dunmurry	Antrim	1804	Commerce	--
McGranaghan	Charles	--			Killygordon	(*)	1847	Hershell	Derry
McGranahan	Patrick	--			Killygordon	(*)	1847	Hershell	Derry
McGrath	Thomas	--	Margaret	--	--	--	1811	Mary	Derry
			James	--					
McGraw	John	--			Strabane	Tyrone	1850	Superior	Derry
McGrenan	John	18			Taughblane	Down	1803	Mohawk	Derry
McGrorty	Daniel	--			Moville	Donegal	1847	Hershell	Derry
McGrory	Ann	--			Ballygawley	(*)	1849	Garland	Derry
McGrotty	John	--			Coleraine	Derry	1849	Garland	Derry
McGuigan	James	--	Christy	--	Draperstown	Derry	1847	Superior	Derry
			Nancy	--					
			Pat	--					
McGuigan	Patrick	--			Draperstown	Derry	1847	Superior	Derry
McGuire	Charles	--			Enderny	Fermanagh	1847	Allegheny	Derry

(*) See Endnotes

Last Name	First Name	Age	Family	Age	Address	County	Date	Ship	Port
McGuire	Pat	--	Michael	--	Enniskillen	Fermanagh	1847	Venice	Derry
McIlhenny	Alexander	--			Letterkenny	Donegal	1850	Superior	Derry
McIlhenny	Margaret	--			L'Derry	Derry	1847	Hartford	Derry
McIlhenny	Sarah	--	John	1	Portlough	Donegal	1847	Hartford	Derry
McIlhill	Michael	--	Ann	--	Beragh	Tyrone	1847	Montpellier	Derry
McIntire	Abraham	--			--	--	1811	Mary	Derry
McIntyre	George	--	Eliza	--	Coleraine	Derry	1849	Superior	Derry
			Alexander	12					
			Margaret	10					
			Jane	8					
			Isabella	6					
			Mary	4					
McIntyre	Isabella	--			Coleraine	Derry	1849	Superior	Derry
McIntyre	Jane	--			Coleraine	Derry	1847	MaryStewart	Derry
McKany	Catherine	--	Ellen	--	N'tnstewart	Tyrone	1847	Venice	Derry
			Owen	10					
McKarry	Alex	--			N'tnstewart	Tyrone	1847	Venice	Derry
McKay	Charles	--			--	--	1811	Harmony	Derry
McKee	Anton	--			Glenwinny	Fermanagh	1847	Barbara	Derry
McKee	Henry	--	Margaret	--	Coleraine	Derry	1850	Superior	Derry
			Sarah	10					
			James	7					
			Andrew	6m					
McKeenan	Moses	--			Coleraine	Derry	1847	MaryStewart	Derry
McKeever	John	--			Maghera	Donegal	1848	HannahKerr	Derry
McKeever	Nancy	45			--	--	1804	Maria	Derry
McKelvey	Margaret	--			N'tnstewart	Tyrone	1850	Envoy	Derry
McKelvey	Sally	--			Stranorlar	Donegal	1850	Envoy	Derry
McKenna	Mary	--			Draperstown	Derry	1850	Superior	Derry
McKenny	John	--	Mary	--	Aghadowey	Derry	1847	Venice	Derry
McKey	Patrick	38			Drumgoland	Down	1803	George	Belfast
McKinlay	Susan	--			Fountainhill	(*)	1849	Garland	Derry

(*) See Endnotes

ULSTER EMIGRANTS TO PHILADELPHIA

Last Name	First Name	Age	Family	Age	Address	County	Date	Ship	Port
McKinley	James	23			--	--	1804	Maria	Derry
McKinley	Jane	--	Esther	--	Convoy	Donegal	1848	HannahKerr	Derry
			Matty	--					
			Elizabeth	6					
			Margaret	5					
McKinley	Margaret	--			Omagh	Tyrone	1850	Superior	Derry
McKinley	Samuel	33			--	--	1804	Maria	Derry
McKinlwy	Hugh	--			--	--	1811	Fame	Derry
McKinna	Mary	--	Margaret	--	Maghera	Donegal	1850	Superior	Derry
McKinner	James	--	Ann	--	Beragh	Tyrone	1850	Envoy	Derry
McKinney	John	--			Drumquin	Tyrone	1850	Envoy	Derry
McKinney	Sarah	--			Limavady	Derry	1847	Allegheny	Derry
McKnight	David	--	Mary	--	--	--	1811	Mary	Derry
			Andrew	--					
			Jane	--					
			Thomas	--					
			Daniel	--					
McLamont	Eliza Ann	--			Coleraine	Derry	1849	Superior	Derry
McLancy	Cormick	5	Daniel	3	Culdaff	Donegal	1850	Superior	Derry
McLaughlan	Sarah	--			Kilmacrenan	Donegal	1847	MaryStewart	Derry
McLaughlin	Bernard	--			Moville	Donegal	1849	Envoy	Derry
McLaughlin	Bernard	--	Catherine	--	Letterkenny	Donegal	1847	Barbara	Derry
McLaughlin	Bridget	--			Malin	Donegal	1850	Envoy	Derry
McLaughlin	Bridget	--	Dennis	2	Malin	Donegal	1848	MaryCampbell	Derry
			Catherine	6m					
McLaughlin	Catherine	--			Clondermott	Derry	1850	Envoy	Derry
McLaughlin	Charles	--	Susan	--	Carne	Donegal	1850	Lumley	Derry
McLaughlin	Eleanor	--			--	--	1811	Harmony	Derry
McLaughlin	Ellen	--			Lisdillon	Derry	1850	Superior	Derry
McLaughlin	Francis	--	Biddy	--	--	--	1811	Harmony	Derry
McLaughlin	George	--	Rosan	--	Limavady	Derry	1847	Hartford	Derry
McLaughlin	H.	--			--	--	1811	Fame	Derry
McLaughlin	Hugh	--			Malin	Donegal	1847	Hershell	Derry

Last Name	First Name	Age	Family	Age	Address	County	Date	Ship	Port
McLaughlin	James	--	Nancy	--	Glengivney ?	?	1847	Allegheny	Derry
			James	--					
			Ann	--					
			Catherine	--					
McLaughlin	James	--	Sarah	--	L'Derry	Derry	1848	HannahKerr	Derry
			Sarah	9m					
McLaughlin	John	--			Carne	Donegal	1850	Envoy	Derry
McLaughlin	John	--			Moville	Donegal	1850	Superior	Derry
McLaughlin	John	--	Elleanor	--	Cumber	Derry	1847	Hershell	Derry
			Biddy	4					
McLaughlin	John	--	John	--	Magilligan	Derry	1847	Allegheny	Derry
McLaughlin	Manny	--			Muff	Derry	1849	Garland	Derry
McLaughlin	Mary	--			Ballygorman	Donegal	1849	Superior	Derry
McLaughlin	Mary	--			Limavady	Derry	1847	MaryStewart	Derry
McLaughlin	Mary	--			Moville	Donegal	1850	Superior	Derry
McLaughlin	Mary	--			St.Johnstown	Donegal	1847	Superior	Derry
McLaughlin	Michael	--			Malin	Donegal	1847	Venice	Derry
McLaughlin	Nancy	--			Carnaghan	Donegal	1850	Envoy	Derry
McLaughlin	Nancy	--			Limavady	Derry	1847	Allegheny	Derry
McLaughlin	Neal	--			Learmount	Derry	1847	Hershell	Derry
McLaughlin	Patrick	--			Feeny	Derry	1850	Envoy	Derry
McLaughlin	Sally	--	Daniel	12	Carne	Donegal	1850	Lumley	Derry
			Elleanor	6					
			Magy	4					
McLaughlin	Sarah	--			Caw	Donegal	1847	Barbara	Derry
McLaughlin	Thomas	--	Rosey	--	Learmount	Derry	1847	Hershell	Derry
McLeon	Patrick	--			--	--	1811	Mary	Derry
McLester	Dennis	--			Coleraine	Derry	1849	Garland	Derry
McLorten	Terrence	--	Catherine	--	--	--	1811	Mary	Derry
McLoughlin	Patrick	32	R.	24	Innishannon	Donegal	1804	Brothers	Derry
McMackin	Ann	--			Dromore	(*)	1849	Envoy	Derry
McManamin	Elizabeth	--			Laghy	Donegal	1847	Hershell	Derry

(*) See Endnotes

Last Name	First Name	Age	Family	Age	Address	County	Date	Ship	Port
McManus	Mary	20	Catherine	18	Terrydremont	Derry	1833-34	--	Derry
McMeekin	Alexander	21			--	--	1803	Edward	Belfast
McMenamin	Ann	--			Castlederg	Tyrone	1848	MaryCampbell	Derry
McMenamin	Catherine	--			Strabane	Tyrone	1850	Superior	Derry
McMenamin	Grace	--			Castlederg	Tyrone	1850	Superior	Derry
McMenamin	James	--			Killygordon	(*)	1847	Barbara	Derry
McMenamin	James	--	Sarah	5	Castlederg	Tyrone	1847	Allegheny	Derry
			John	3					
			Margaret	1					
			Hugh	--					
McMenamin	John	--			Letterkenny	Donegal	1847	Barbara	Derry
McMenamin	John	--			Strabane	Tyrone	1850	Superior	Derry
McMenamin	Rose	--			Dunnamanagh	Derry	1850	Superior	Derry
McMenamin	William	--			Castlefin	Donegal	1847	Hershell	Derry
McMichael	James	--			Ballycastle	Derry	1847	Venice	Derry
McMillan	Isaac	20			Ardina	Derry	1833	--	Derry
McMillen	Jane	--			Ture	Donegal	1849	Garland	Derry
McMulkin	John	--			Lowtherstown	Fermanagh	1849	Garland	Derry
McMullan	Eliza	--	Cornelius	3	Coleraine	Derry	1847	Barbara	Derry
McNabb	Mathew	--	Mary	--	Coleraine	Derry	1848	MaryCampbell	Derry
McNamee	James	--			Gortin	(*)	1847	Montpellier	Derry
McNamee	Teague	--			Letterkenny	Donegal	1847	Venice	Derry
McNaught	John	--	Glen	--	Draperstown	Derry	1850	Superior	Derry
McNeal	Roger	--			--	--	1811	Harmony	Derry
McNeal	William	--			N'tnstewart	Tyrone	1850	Lumley	Derry
McNicholl	James	--			Garvagh	Derry	1847	Venice	Derry
McNicholl	Patrick	--			Garvagh	Derry	1849	Superior	Derry
McNutt	Matty	--			Carrygalt	Donegal	1847	Barbara	Derry
McPartlan	Hugh	23	Mary	22	Ballyshannon	Donegal	1804	Jefferson	Bally-shannon
McPike	Bridget	--			Beragh	Tyrone	1847	Superior	Derry
McQuade	Arthur	--			Coleraine	Derry	1847	Venice	Derry

(*) See Endnotes

Last Name	First Name	Age	Family	Age	Address	County	Date	Ship	Port
McQuade	Arthur	--			Coleraine	Derry	1848	HannahKerr	Derry
McQuade	BIddy	--			Baronscourt	Tyrone	1847	Barbara	Derry
McQuade	Edward	--			Enniskillen	Fermanagh	1847	Montpellier	Derry
McQuade	Nelis	--			Dromore	(*)	1849	Garland	Derry
McQuaid	John	--	Mary	--	Baronscourt	Tyrone	1848	MaryCampbell	Derry
			James	--					
			Michael	--					
			Sarah	11					
			Catherine	9					
McQuillan	Margaret	--			Letterkenny	Donegal	1847	Venice	Derry
McQuillan	Martha	--			Coleraine	Derry	1850	Envoy	Derry
McQuiston	Robert	26			Dungiven	Derry	1803	Mohawk	Derry
McRanald	John	--	Mary	--	Limavady	Derry	1850	Envoy	Derry
			John	--					
			Michael	12					
			Nancy	10					
			Catherine	7					
			Patrick	4					
McRye	Margaret	--			Dunfanaghy	Donegal	1850	Envoy	Derry
McShane	Thomas	--			--	--	1811	Harmony	Derry
McShea	Mary	--	James	--	Ballybofey	Donegal	1848	HannahKerr	Derry
McSheffry	Hugh	--			Moville	Donegal	1847	Hershell	Derry
McSparran	Arch.	40	M.H.	35	Drumramer	Derry	1833-34	--	Derry
McSwigan	Bernard	--			Omagh	Tyrone	1848	MaryCampbell	Derry
McSwigan	Ellen	--			Beragh	Tyrone	1849	Superior	Derry
McSwine	Hugh	--			Buncrana	Donegal	1847	Venice	Derry
McTaggart	Patrick	--			Ramelton	Donegal	1850	Lumley	Derry
McTogart	Mrs.	--	& Family	--	--	--	1811	Fame	Derry
McVey	Charles	--	Susan	--	Dungiven	Derry	1848	HannahKerr	Derry
			John	11					
			George	9					
			Sarah	7					
			Susan	5					

Last Name	First Name	Age	Family	Age	Address	County	Date	Ship	Port
(Cont'd.)			MaryJane	2					
			Charles	6m					
McWar	James	--			Carne	Donegal	1850	Superior	Derry
McWilliams	Cathrine	--			Beragh	Tyrone	1849	Superior	Derry
Meahan	Mary	--			Beragh	Tyrone	1847	Hartford	Derry
Meenan	Peggy	--			Rosnakill	Donegal	1849	Garland	Derry
Mehaffy	Margaret	--	James	12	Castlederg	Tyrone	1849	Envoy	Derry
			John	10					
			Patrick	8					
			Charles	6					
			Edward	4					
Mellon	James	23			Oughtymore	Derry	1833-34	--	Derry
Mellon	John	--	Elizabeth	--	Castlederg	Tyrone	1848	MaryCampbell	Derry
Mellon	Susan	--	Margaret	1	Clogher	(*)	1847	Montpellier	Derry --
Menagh	Alexander	--	Rebecca	--	Dungiven	Derry	1848	MaryCampbell	Derry
			Marg.Eliza.	9m					
Menagh	Michael	--	Biddy	--	Omagh	Tyrone	1847	Venice	Derry
			Ann	13					
			Margaret	10					
			Daniel	8					
			Elliot	6					
			Pat	3					
			Biddy	9m					
Miley	John	45			Enniskillen	Fermanagh	1803	Strafford	Derry
Millar	Robert	26			--	--	1804	Maria	Derry
Millen	Jane	--	Samuel	--	Coleraine	Derry	1849	Superior	Derry
Millen	Magy	--	Eliza	--	Coleraine	Derry	1849	Garland	Derry
Miller	Andrew	--	Rebecca	--	Ardstraw	Tyrone	1850	Envoy	Derry
Miller	Catherine	--			Castlefin	Donegal	1848	MaryCampbell	Derry
Miller	Catherine	--			Claudy	Derry	1847	Barbara	Derry
Miller	James	--			Raphoe	Donegal	1847	Superior	Derry
Miller	John	--			Cross	(*)	1850	Superior	Derry

(*) See Endnotes

Last Name	First Name	Age	Family	Age	Address	County	Date	Ship	Port
Miller	John	21			Coleraine	Derry	1833	--	Derry
Miller	John	21	Margaret	18	Tullans	Derry	1833-34	--	Derry
Miller	Mary Jane	--	Ann	--	Banagher	Fermanagh	1847	Superior	Derry
Miller	Thomas	--	Martha	--	Claudy	Derry	1847	Montpellier	Derry
			James	6					
			John	4					
			William	1					
Millon	Jane	--			Limavady	Derry	1847	Venice	Derry
Mills	Andrew	--			--	--	1811	Mary	Derry
Mills	Jane	--			St.Johnston	Donegal	1848	HannahKerr	Derry
Mills	Robert	40			--	--	1803	Active	Newry
Mitchell	James	22			L'Derry	Derry	1803	Penna.	Derry
Mitchell	John	--	James	--	Fahan	Donegal	1847	Hartford	Derry
Mitchell	Mary	--			Drumskellen	Donegal	1847	Superior	Derry
Mitchell	Mary	--			L'Derry	Derry	1848	HannahKerr	Derry
Mitchell	Sarah	25			Loughinisland	Down	1804	Commerce	--
Mitchell	Thomas	--	MaryAnne	--	Gobnascale	Donegal	1849	Garland	Derry
			Anne	--					
			Sarah	12					
			Ellen	8					
			MaryJane	6					
			Christian	3					
Mitchell	William	--	Sarah	--	Cloughfin	Derry	1847	Hartford	Derry
Mitchell	William	20			Cumber	Derry	1803	Strafford	Derry
Mogie	Jane	--			Coleraine	Derry	1847	MaryStewart	Derry
Monaghan	Ann	--			Pettigoe	(*)	1849	Envoy	Derry
Monegan	Charles	--	Mary (W)	--	Millford	Donegal	1847	Superior	Derry
Monegan	Francis	--			--	--	1811	Mary	Derry
Monegle	Patrick	--			Ramelton	Donegal	1847	Montpellier	Derry
Monks	Thomas	60	Robert	22	--	--	1803	Edward	Belfast
			Joseph	20					
Monteith	George	--	Mary Jane	--	Lisnacloon	Tyrone	1850	Envoy	Derry

(*) See Endnotes

Last Name	First Name	Age	Family	Age	Address	County	Date	Ship	Port
Monteith	Samuel	--	Rebecca	--	Castlederg	Tyrone	1850	Envoy	Derry
Montgomery	May	41			L'Derry	Derry	1803	Penna.	Derry
Montgomery	Rebecca	10			Ballindrait	Donegal	1803	Penna.	Derry
Montgomery	Samuel	12			L'Derry	Derry	1803	Penna.	Derry
Montgomery	Sarah	--			Waterside	Derry	1847	Barbara	Derry
Montgomery	William	--	Margaret	--	Waterside	Derry	1847	Allegheny	Derry
Montgomery	William	22			L'Derry	Derry	1803	Penna.	Derry
Moon	Edward	20			Clarkhill	Derry	1834	--	Derry
Moon	John	24			Clarkhill	Derry	1834	--	Derry
Moon	Jonathan	24			Clarkhill	Derry	1834	--	Derry
Mooney	James	16			--	--	1803	Edward	Belfast
Mooney	John	--			Ramelton	Donegal	1849	Envoy	Derry
Mooney	Martha	--			Coleraine	Derry	1849	Superior	Derry
Mooney	William	--	Hannah	--	Fintona	Tyrone	1847	Allegheny	Derry
			William	--					
			Hannah	--					
			Rebecca	11					
Moore	Alexander	--	Catherine	--	Rossgole	Fermanagh	1847	Allegheny	Derry
			Peter	--					
			Matty	2					
Moore	Alexander	--	Jane	--	Coleraine	Derry	1847	Allegheny	Derry
			William	--					
			Rebecca	--					
Moore	David	--			Letterkenny	Donegal	1850	Envoy	Derry
Moore	James	19			Ballykelly	Derry	1803	Strafford	Derry
Moore	James	21			--	--	1803	Active	Newry
Moore	John	19			Loughlin	Donegal	1803	Strafford	Derry
Moore	John	20			Bovevagh	Derry	1833-34	--	Derry
Moore	John	22			Limavady	Derry	1803	Penna.	Derry
Moore	Margaret	--	William	--	Beragh	Tyrone	1847	Superior	Derry
			Ann	--					

(*) See Endnotes

Last Name	First Name	Age	Family	Age	Address	County	Date	Ship	Port
(Cont'd.)			Mary	--					
			Thomas	10					
Moore	Peggy	--	Martha	--	Fanad	Donegal	1847	Superior	Derry
Moore	Rebecca	--			Drumahoe	Derry	1850	Envoy	Derry
Moore	Richard	--			Kilmacrenan	Donegal	1849	Garland	Derry
Moore	Robert	--			--	--	1847	Hershell	Derry
Moore	Verner	--	Rebecca	--	Banagher	Fermanagh	1847	Superior	Derry
Moore	William	--			--	--	1811	Harmony	Derry
Moore	William	--			Coleraine	Derry	1847	Superior	Derry
Moorhead	Alexander	--			Convoy	Donegal	1850	Lumley	Derry
Moorhead	Margaret	--			Magilligan	Derry	1847	Allegheny	Derry
Moran	James	--			N'tnstewart	Tyrone	1850	Envoy	Derry
Moren	Philip	--	Catherine	--	Beragh	Tyrone	1850	Superior	Derry
			Ann	--					
			James	--					
Morrin	Edward	--	Sarah	--	Ballybofey	Donegal	1848	HannahKerr	Derry
Morris	Bernard	--	Isabella	--	Plumbridge	Derry	1847	Superior	Derry
Morris	Catherine	--	Mary	--	Letterkenny	Donegal	1847	Venice	Derry
Morris	Nancy	--			Gortin	(*)	1849	Envoy	Derry
Morris	William	--			N'tnstewart	Tyrone	1849	Superior	Derry
Morrison	Elizabeth	--			--	--	1811	Mary	Derry
Morrison	Hugh	--			L'Derry	Derry	1850	Superior	Derry
Morrison	Matilda	--			Gallan	Tyrone	1849	Superior	Derry
Morrison	T. White	20	J. White	18	Drumore	Derry	1833-34	--	Derry
Morrow	George	28			Bushmills	Antrim	1803	Brutus	Derry
Morrow	Henry	--			Elagh	Tyrone	1849	Superior	Derry
Moss	John	--	Catherine	--	Omagh	Tyrone	1850	Superior	Derry
			John	12					
			Sally	10					
			Mary Ann	8					
Mossey	Mary	--			Omagh	Tyrone	1847	Hartford	Derry
Moyne	William	--	Catherine	--	Castlefin	Donegal	1847	Allegheny	Derry

(*) See Endnotes

ULSTER EMIGRANTS TO PHILADELPHIA

Last Name	First Name	Age	Family	Age	Address	County	Date	Ship	Port
Mulberry	Robert	--	Martha	--	L'Derry	Derry	1849	Superior	Derry
			James	10					
			Mary Jane	8					
			Rebecca	4					
			Martha	2					
			Eliza	3m					
			Jane	--					
Mulden	Anthony	--			--	--	1811	Mary	Derry
Mulherrin	Charles	--			Dunfanaghy	Donegal	1850	Lumley	Derry
Mullan	Biddy	--			Garvagh	Derry	1847	Venice	Derry
Mullan	Mary	--			Limavady	Derry	1849	Garland	Derry
Mullan	Nancy	--			Feeny	Derry	1850	Envoy	Derry
Mullan	Patrick	21			Tynan	Armagh	1803	George	Belfast
Mullan	Thomas	--			Muff	Derry	1849	Garland	Derry
Mullen	Charles	--	James	--	N'tnstewart	Tyrone	1847	Hershell	Derry
			Rosanna	--					
Mullen	James	40	Sarah	40	Drumreighlin	Derry	1833-34--		Derry
			Ann	10					
			Margaret	8					
			Jane	6					
			Sally	4					
Mullen	Margaret	--			L'Derry	Derry	1847	Barbara	Derry
Mullen	Nancy	--			Dunnyboe	Tyrone	1848	HannahKerr	Derry
Mullen	Susan	--	John	--	Beragh	Tyrone	1847	Superior	Derry
			Thomas	--					
			Betty	--					
Mullen	Thomas	25	John	30	Mullaghmore	Derry	1834	--	Derry
			Bernard	23					
			Catherine	22					
			John	30					
Mullins	John	--	Biddy	--	Limavady	Derry	1850	Envoy	Derry
			Andrew	--					
			Catherine	--					

Last Name	First Name	Age	Family	Age	Address	County	Date	Ship	Port
(Cont'd.)			Nancy	12					
			Biddy	10					
			Ellen	8					
			Grace	6					
			Mary	3					
			James	3m					
Munay	Margaret	--	Rebecca	--	Limavady	Derry	1848	HannahKerr	Derry
Munn	Catherine	--			Dooey	(*)	1850	Superior	Derry
Murphy	Arthur	49			--	--	1804	Maria	Derry
Murphy	Hugh	18			--	--	1803	Edward	Belfast
Murphy	John	--			Coleraine	Derry	1849	Envoy	Derry
Murphy	Joseph	--			Coleraine	Derry	1849	Garland	Derry
Murphy	Lawrence	--	Margaret	--	N'tnstewart	Tyrone	1847	Allegheny	Derry
			Elizabeth	--					
			Sarah	--					
			Andrew	12					
			Ann	10					
Murphy	Mary Ann	--	Lavey	--	Dungannon	Tyrone	1850	Superior	Derry
Murphy	Patrick	30			L'Derry	Derry	1803	Brutus	Derry
Murphy	Sarah	21			--	--	1804	Maria	Derry
Murphy	Thomas	26			L'Derry	Derry	1803	Brutus	Derry
Murray	Ann	--	Catherine	7	Strabane	Tyrone	1847	Superior	Derry
			Rosannah	4					
Murray	James	20			Dunnamanagh	Derry	1803	Mohawk	Derry
Murray	Michael	--			SixMileCross	Tyrone	1847	Barbara	Derry
Murtland	Elizabeth	--	John	--	Limavady	Derry	1849	Garland	Derry
			Elizabeth	--					
			Roseanna	--					
			James	11					
			MaryJane	8					
			Daniel	5					
			Joseph	2					

(*) See Endnotes

ULSTER EMIGRANTS TO PHILADELPHIA

Last Name	First Name	Age	Family	Age	Address	County	Date	Ship	Port
Murtlen	Betty	--			Derg Beg	Donegal	1848	MaryCampbell	Derry
Nanson	Mathew	--			--	--	1811	Harmony	Derry
Nash	Donald	26			Clanely	Tyrone	1803	Penna.	Derry
Neely	Williiam	55	Jane	40	Ballynary	Derry	1833-34	--	Derry
			James	20					
			William	15					
			John	25					
			Mary Ann	22					
Neill	Martha	--	Eliza	--	Coleraine	Derry	1849	Envoy	Derry
Neill	William	--	Margaret	--	Coleraine	Derry	1847	Superior	Derry
Neilly	Joseph	24			Ballynary	Derry	1833-34	--	Derry
Neilson	James	--			--	--	1811	Fame	Derry
Neily	Eacy	20			Largy	Derry	1833-34	--	Derry
Nelis	Ann	--			L'Derry	Derry	1848	HannahKerr	Derry
Nelis	Henry	--	Margaret	--	Raphoe	Donegal	1849	Envoy	Derry
			Hugh	--					
			Elleanor	12					
			Matilda	10					
			John	5					
			Timothy	2					
Nelis	John	--			L'Derry	Derry	1847	Hartford	Derry
Nelis	Margy	--			L'Derry	Derry	1850	Superior	Derry
Nelson	James	28			--	Down	1803	Patty	Newry
Nelson	Margaret	--	Sarah	--	Castlederg	Tyrone	1848	MaryCampbell	Derry
Nelson	Wilson	--			Buncrana	Donegal	1848	HannahKerr	Derry
Nicholl	David	--			Fahan	Donegal	1847	Hartford	Derry
Niely	Elizabeth	21			Newton	Donegal	1803	Mohawk	Derry
Nilson	Daniel	--			Fanad	Donegal	1850	Envoy	Derry
Nimmock	Eliza	--			Coleraine	Derry	1849	Garland	Derry
Norris	John	16			--	--	1803	Edward	Belfast
Norris	Mary	--			--	--	1811	Harmony	Derry
Norris	Robert	--	Mary	--	--	--	1811	Mary	Derry
Nowry	James	--	Alexander	8	Coleraine	Derry	1849	Garland	Derry
			Elizabeth	6					

ULSTER EMIGRANTS TO PHILADELPHIA

Last Name	First Name	Age	Family	Age	Address	County	Date	Ship	Port
Nugent	Patrick	--			Cappagh	Donegal	1847	Hartford	Derry
O'Brien	Barny	--	Henry	--	Crossroads	Donegal	1847	Montpellier	Derry
O'Brien	Margaret	--	Martha	12	Chruchill	Donegal	1850	Envoy	Derry
			Matthew	9					
			George	1					
O'Brien	Sophia	--	Harry	--	Crossroads	Donegal	1847	Montpellier	Derry
O'Brien	Sarah	--			Castlederg	Tyrone	1848	MaryCampbell	Derry
O'Donnel	Michael	--	Sarah	--	Moville	Donegal	1847	Venice	Derry
O'Donnell	Charles	--	Lily	--	Letterkenny	Donegal	1847	Superior	Derry
			John	4					
			James	2					
O'Donnell	John	--	Jane	--	Castlefin	Donegal	1847	Superior	Derry
			Dominick	12					
			Edward	10					
			John	8					
			Margaret	6					
			Charles	4					
			James	2					
O'Donnell	Martha	--			L'Derry	Derry	1848	HannahKerr	Derry
O'Donnell	Mary	25			Strabane	Tyrone	1803	Penna.	Derry
O'Kane	Dennis	33	Jane	--	Edenreabeg	Derry	1844	--	Derry
			Jane	13					
			Rosa	11					
			John	9					
			Dennis,	3					
O'Neill	Francis	27	Emilia	22	--	Dublin	1804	Commerce	--
O'Neill	John	--	Mary	--	Lowtherstown	Fermanagh	1847	Hartford	Derry
Orr	James	30	Jane	32	Cullyapple	Derry	1834	--	Derry
			Margaret	11					
			Elizabeth	9					
			Ann	5					

(*) See Endnotes

Last Name	First Name	Age	Family	Age	Address	County	Date	Ship	Port
(Cont'd.)			Isabella	7					
			Hannah	3					
Orr	Joshua	--			--	--	1811	Fame	Derry
Orr	Mary Jane	--	Nancy	--	Coleraine	Derry	1849	Garland	Derry
Orr	Matty	--	Eliza	--	Clondermot	Derry	1847	Venice	Derry
Orr	Robert	--			--	--	1811	Fame	Derry
Orr	Robert	--	Hannah	--	Claudy	Derry	1847	Montpellier	Derry
Osberg	John	17			Lisnamuck	Derry	1833-34	--	Derry
Osburne	Margaret	27	Jane	6	Omagh	Tyrone	1804	Brothers	Derry
			James	4					
Paisley	Mary	--			Omagh	Tyrone	1850	Envoy	Derry
Parker	William	50			Dungiven	Derry	1803	Penna.	Derry
Parkhill	Margaret	--			Kilmacrenan	Donegal	1847	MaryStewart	Derry
Parnell	Martha	18			--	--	1803	Active	Newry
Patterson	Elizabeth	25			Clintagh	Derry	1833-34	--	Derry
Patterson	Joseph	62			Clintagh	Derry	1833-34	--	Derry
Patterson	Mary	26			Clintagh	Derry	1833-34	--	Derry
Patterson	Richard	43			Clintagh	Derry	1833-34	--	Derry
Patterson	Samuel	--			--	--	1811	Harmony	Derry
Patterson	Samuel	33			Clintagh	Derry	1833-34	--	Derry
Patton	James	--	Ellen	--	Coleraine	Derry	1849	Envoy	Derry
Patton	Mary	--			Ballymoney	Antrim	1850	Superior	Derry
Patton	Mary	--	Martha Jane	--	Ballymoney	Antrim	1850	Lumley	Derry
Patton	Mathew	--	John	--	Coleraine	Derry	1849	Garland	Derry
Patton	Samuel	32	Joseph	36	--	Down	1803	Patty	Newry
Pauley	John	--			Beragh	Tyrone	1849	Superior	Derry
Pearson	Margaret	52			--	--	1804	Maria	Derry
Peoples	James	--			Ramelton	Donegal	1849	Envoy	Derry
Peoples	James	23			Letterkenny	Donegal	1803	Brutus	Derry
Peoples	Joana	--			Ramelton	Donegal	1847	Barbara	Derry
Peoples	Margaret	--	Samuel	--	Ramelton	Donegal	1849	Superior	Derry
Perry	Betty	--	Matilda	--	Garvagh	Derry	1847	Venice	Derry
Philips	Abraham	35			Urney	Tyrone	1803	Mohawk	Derry

ULSTER EMIGRANTS TO PHILADELPHIA

Last Name	First Name	Age	Family	Age	Address	County	Date	Ship	Port
Piper	William	22			Corndale	Derry	1833-34--		Derry
Pollock	Ann	--			Carndonagh	Donegal	1850	Envoy	Derry
Pollock	Mary	--			Cross	(*)	1849	Superior	Derry
Pollock	Thomas	--			Coleraine	Derry	1849	Superior	Derry
Porter	Harvey	--			L'Derry	Derry	1850	Envoy	Derry
Porter	Hugh	24			--	--	1803	Edward	Belfast
Porter	James	35			Beefan	Donegal	1804	Brothers	Derry
Porter	John	43	Elitia	44	Lochris	Donegal	1804	Catherine	Bally-shannon
			Catherine	22					
			William	20					
			Alexander	18					
Porter	William	--			L'Derry	Derry	1847	Venice	Derry
Potts	Walter	25			--	Down	1803	Patty	Newry
Preston	Cherry	--			Elaghmore	Derry	1849	Envoy	Derry
Preston	Robert	--			Elagh	Tyrone	1849	Envoy	Derry
Price	Ann	--			Rathmullan	Donegal	1849	Garland	Derry
Proctor	Alexander	40			Knocknogher	Derry	1833	--	Derry
Pumphy	John	29			Belfast	Antrim	1803	George	Belfast
Purdy	Nancy	--			Articlave	Derry	1850	Envoy	Derry
ꞏQuigg	John	--			Moville	Donegal	1847	Hershell	Derry
Quigley	Andrew	--	Roseann	--	Elagh	Tyrone	1849	Superior	Derry
Quigley	Martha	--			--	--	1811	Fame	Derry
Quigley	Rebecca	--			Moville	Donegal	1850	Envoy	Derry
Quigley	Sarah	--			Fahan	Donegal	1850	Superior	Derry
Quin	Charles	--			--	--	1811	Fame	Derry
Quin	Margaret	--	Susannah	--	Ballybofey	Donegal	1848	HannahKerr	Derry
Quinn	Bridget	--			Monksfield	Galway	1847	Barbara	Derry
Rafferty	John	--	Ann	--	Monksfield	Galway	1847	Venice	Derry
Ralston	Anne	34	Anne	2	--	Tyrone	1803	Strafford	Derry
			Robert	19					
			David	15					

(*) See Endnotes

77

Last Name	First Name	Age	Family	Age	Address	County	Date	Ship	Port
(Cont'd.)			John	11					
			Jane	8					
			Anne	5					
			Josh	2					
Ralston	James	45	Mary	40	--	Tyrone	1803	Strafford	Derry
			James	15					
			Mary	12					
			David	9					
			Josh	5					
Ralston	John	40	Sarah	40	--	Tyrone	1803	Strafford	Derry
			David	9					
			Andrew	7					
			William	3					
			James	5					
Ramsay	Robert	--			Dungiven	Derry	1848	HannahKerr	Derry
Rankin	Henry	17			--	--	1804	Maria	Derry
Rankin	Hugh	16			Blagh	Derry	1833	--	Derry
Rankin	John	--			Letterkenny	Donegal	1850	Envoy	Derry
Rankin	Robert	--			--	--	1811	Harmony	Derry
Rankin	William	18			Blagh	Derry	1833	--	Derry
Raulstone	Archibald	--			--	--	1811	Mary	Derry
Ray	Robert	18			Knocknogher	Derry	1834	--	Derry
Rea	John	--			--	--	1811	Harmony	Derry
Rea	John	20			Glenconway	Derry	1833-34	--	Derry
Read	James	23			--	--	1803	Edward	Belfast
Reed	Ellen	--			Churchill	Donegal	1847	Hartford	Derry
Reed	James	--			--	--	1811	Fame	Derry
Reed	Jane	--			Strabane	Tyrone	1847	MaryStewart	Derry
Reed	Margaret	--			Kilmacrenan	Donegal	1847	MaryStewart	Derry
Reed	Margaret Ann	--			Coleraine	Derry	1847	Hershell	Derry
Reid	Alexander	--			Ballybofey	Donegal	1848	HannahKerr	Derry
Reid	Robert	60	Ann	55	Aghadowey	Derry	1833-34	--	Derry
			John	21					

Last Name	First Name	Age	Family	Age	Address	County	Date	Ship	Port
(Cont'd.)			Miss	16					
			' Esther	10					
			Sarah	52					
			Levy	16					
Reilly	Thomas	--			Enniskillen	Fermanagh	1848	MaryCampbell	Derry
Rein	John	--			--	--	1811	Mary	Derry
Rendles	James	40	John	38	--	--	1803	Active	Newry
			Elizabeth	16					
			Thomas	12					
Rennie	Sarah	--			Coleraine	Derry	1850	Superior	Derry
Rice	John	38			--	--	1804	Maria	Derry
Riddells	Charles	40	Elizabeth	41	Lisnamuck	Derry	1833-34	--	Derry
			Hugh	2					
			Robert	4					
			Charles	20					
			Matty	22					
			William	12					
			Matilda	10					
			Samuel	8					
			Margaret	6					
			Robert	64					
			MaryAnn	60					
Riddle	Elizabeth	--			Coleraine	Derry	1849	Garland	Derry
Robb	Samuel	--	Richard	11	Ramelton	Donegal	1849	Garland	Derry
			Eliza	8					
			John	6					
			Margaret	3					
Robinson	Ann	22			Innishannon	Donegal	1804	Brothers	Derry
Robinson	Ann	7			Ramelton	Donegal	1849	Garland	Derry
Robinson	Peggy	--			Draperstown	Derry	1847	Montpellier	Derry
Robinson	Sarah	--	David	6	Letterkenny	Donegal	1847	Venice	Derry
			Catherine	9					
Robinson	William	32			Coleraine	Derry	1804	Brothers	Derry

ULSTER EMIGRANTS TO PHILADELPHIA

Last Name	First Name	Age	Family	Age	Address	County	Date	Ship	Port
Robsinson	Mary Ann	--			Londonderry	Derry	1847	Hershell	Derry
Rodden	Manus	--			Letterkenny	Donegal	1849	Envoy	Derry
Rodden	Peggy	--			Malin	Donegal	1850	Superior	Derry
Rodder	Michael	--			--	--	1811	Harmony	Derry
Roddy	Hugh	--	Jane	--	Dunkineely	Tyrone	1850	Superior	Derry
			James	9					
			Denis	6					
			Mary	4					
			John	1					
			Patrick	12					
Rodgers	Catherine	--			Castlefin	Donegal	1848	MaryCampbell	Derry
Rodgers	Francis	--	James	--	Castelderg	Tyrone	1849	Envoy	Derry
			Mary	--					
			Elleanor	--					
Rodgers	Mathew	--			Castlefin	Donegal	1848	MaryCampbell	Derry
Rodgers	Samuel	--			--	--	1811	Fame	Derry
Rodgers	Thomas	--	Susan	--	Castlederg	Tyrone	1847	Hartford	Derry
Rogers	James	--			Newbuildings	(*)	1849	Garland	Derry
Rogers	Mary Ann	--			Ballymoney	Antrim	1850	Superior	Derry
Rogers	Nathan	--			--	--	1811	Mary	Derry
Roney	William	19			--	Down	1803	Patty	Newry
Ross	David	24			Gortnarne	Derry	1833-34	--	Derry
Ross	David	24	Jane	26	Lislane	Derry	1833-34	--	Derry
Ross	Joseph	--	Eleanor	--	--	--	1811	Mary	Derry
Ross	Robert	--			Coleraine	Derry	1849	Superior	Derry
Ross	William	--			--	--	1811	Mary	Derry
Roulstone	Anne	--			St.Johnston	Donegal	1849	Superior	Derry
Roulstone	Harvey	--	Martha	--	--	--	1811	Mary	Derry
			James	--					
Russel	Catherine	--			Millford	Donegal	1847	Allegheny	Derry
Russel	Elizabeth	--			Letterkenny	Donegal	1849	Envoy	Derry
Russel	Ellen	--			Dunnamanagh	Derry	1848	MaryCampbell	Derry

(*) See Endnotes

ULSTER EMIGRANTS TO PHILADELPHIA

Last Name	First Name	Age	Family	Age	Address	County	Date	Ship	Port
Russel	James	--			Churchill	Donegal	1847	Hartford	Derry
Russel	James	--			Elagh	Tyrone	1849	Superior	Derry
Russel	Mary	--	Mary	--	Carnmore	Fermanagh	1848	MaryCampbell	Derry
			Alexander	--					
Russell	JaneEliz.	--			Muff	Derry	1850	Superior	Derry
Ruthedge	Margaret	--			Castlederg	Tyrone	1848	HannahKerr	Derry
Rutherford	Anten	--	Elizabeth	--	Millford	Donegal	1848	MaryCampbell	Derry
			Letitia	3					
			Alexander	2					
Rutherford	John	--	Mary	--	--		1811	Fame	Derry	Sarah
Rutlidge	James	--			Castlederg	Tyrone	1848	HannahKerr	Derry
Sanderson	Thomas	22			Collins	Derry	1833-34–		Derry
Scallon	John	--	Susan	--	Ederny	Fermanagh	1847	Allegheny	Derry
Scollon	Catherine	--			Ederney	Fermanagh	1849	Envoy	Derry
Scott	Archibald	26	Elinor	20	Tullymore	Donegal	1804	Catherine	Bally-shannon
Scott	Elizabeth	--			Gortin	(*)	1850	Envoy	Derry
Scott	Elizabeth	--	Jane	--	Enniskillen	Fermanagh	1850	Superior	Derry
			Eliza	--					
Scott	Francis	47			--	--	1804	Maria	Derry
Scott	John	--	William	--	Glenalla	Donegal	1847	Allegheny	Derry
			John	--					
			James	--					
Scott	Mary		Ann	--	Kilmacrenan	Donegal	1850	Lumley	Derry
Scott	Robert	32	John	30	Aghansillagh	Derry	1833-34 --		Derry
Scott	Sarah	--			Waterside	Derry	1849	Superior	Derry
Scott	William	20			Ardara	Donegal	1804	Catherine	Bally-shannon
Scott	William	22			--	--	1803	Edward	Belfast
Servoce	Thomas	18			Brockaghs	Antrim	1803	George	Belfast
Shannon	Cook	--			Enniskillen	Fermanagh	1847	Venice	Derry
Shannon	John	--			Stranorlar	Donegal	1847	Venice	Derry

(*) See Endnotes

ULSTER EMIGRANTS TO PHILADELPHIA

Last Name	First Name	Age	Family	Age	Address	County	Date	Ship	Port
Sharkey	John	--			Dunlo	Galway	1847	Hartford	Derry
Shaw	Eliza	--			Claudy	Derry	1847	Superior	Derry
Shean	Elinor	60			--	Down	1803	Strafford	Derry
Sheerin	Daniel	24			Ardara	Donegal	1804	Catherine	Bally-shannon
Sheerin	John	--	Ann	--	Strabane	Tyrone	1847	Allegheny	Derry
			Ann	6					
			Eliza	3					
Sheils	Con	--	Catherine	--	Culdaff	Donegal	1848	HannahKerr	Derry
Sheils	Kate	--	Hannah	1	Rosnakill	Donegal	1847	MaryStewart	Derry
			Biddy	--					
Sheils	Michael	--	Magy	--	Rosnakill	Donegal	1847	MaryStewart	Derry
			Ellen	--					
Sherra	John	--			Limavady	Derry	1847	Hartford	Derry
Sherry	John	34			Blaris	Down	1804	Commerce	--
Shiel	Thomas	30			Tullans	Derry	1833-34	--	Derry
Simon	Jane	--			--	--	1811	Fame	Derry
Simpson	John	25			Stewartstown	Tyrone	1803	Mohawk	Derry
Simpson	Mrs.	--			Dunfanaghy	Donegal	1848	MaryCampbell	Derry
Simpson	William	--			Ballyartan	Derry	1847	Superior	Derry
Sinclair	Nancy	9	James	7	Coleraine	Derry	1847	Venice	Derry
Sinyard	Johnathan	--	George	--	Limavady	Derry	1848	HannahKerr	Derry
			Hannah	--					
Size	Bernard	--	Hannah	--	--	--	1811	Harmony	Derry
Smiley	Catherine	--			Clooney	(*)	1847	Venice	Derry
Smiley	John	--			--	--	1811	Harmony	Derry
Smily	James	27			L'Derry	Derry	1803	Brutus	Derry
Smily	William	23			Kereight	Wexford	1803	Strafford	Derry
Smith	Catherine	--			L'Derry	Derry	1848	HannahKerr	Derry
Smith	Daniel	--	Jane	--	Limavady	Derry	1847	Barbara	Derry
			Joseph	--					
			William	--					

(*) See Endnotes

Last Name	First Name	Age	Family	Age	Address	County	Date	Ship	Port
			David	13					
			Martha	12					
Smith	Hannah	--			Glentogher	Donegal	1849	Envoy	Derry
Smith	Hugh	44			--	--	1804	Maria	Derry
Smith	James	--			Limavady	Derry	1848	MaryCampbell	Derry
Smith	James	--	Frances	--	Omagh	Tyrone	1847	Venice	Derry
Smith	John	20			--	--	1803	Edward	Belfast
Smith	John	20			Moneycarris	Derry	1834	--	Derry
Smith	Martha	--			--	--	1811	Mary	Derry
Smith	Martha Jane	--			Dungiven	Derry	1848	HannahKerr	Derry
Smith	Robert	--	Eliza	--	Stranorlar	Donegal	1847	Venice	Derry
			Margaret	13					
			Thomas	11					
			James	8					
			MaryJane	3					
			Hannah	1					
Smith	Robert	23			Ballyscullion	Derry	1833-34--		Derry
Smith	Robert	24			Upr. Drumons	Derry	1833-34 --		Derry
Smith	Samuel	20			Bolea	Derry	1833-34 --		Derry
Smith	Sarah	--			N'tnstewart	Tyrone	1850	Superior	Derry
Smyth	Francis	29			Enniskillen	Fermanagh	1803	Mohawk	Derry
Smyth	George	--			--	--	1811	Fame	Derry
Smyth	Hugh	12	Mary	10	Glentogher	Donegal	1849	Envoy	Derry
			Elleanor	8					
Smyth	Mathew	--			L'Derry	Derry	1847	Superior	Derry
Smyth	Sally Ann	--			Clogher	(*)	1847	Venice	Derry
Speer	Andrew	--			Omagh	Tyrone	1847	Hartford	Derry
Speer	Elizabeth	--			Rossgole	Fermanagh	1847	Allegheny	Derry
Speir	John	--	Hannah	--	Kilmacrenan	Donegal	1847	Hartford	Derry
			Catherine	--					
			Mary	--					
			Rebecca	--					

(*) See Endnotes

Last Name	First Name	Age	Family	Age	Address	County	Date	Ship	Port
(Cont'd.)			Eliz.	--					
			Robert	--					
			Margaret	9					
			Andrew	7					
			Gerred	5					
			Hannah	5					
Sreen	Andrew	--	Jane (W)	--	Racecourse	Galway	1847	Superior	Derry
			Thomas	3					
			Alexander	2					
			Jane	3m					
Stark	Sarah	--			N'tnstewart	Tyrone	1847	Superior	Derry
Starrs	Edward	--			Beragh	Tyrone	1847	Superior	Derry
Steel	Jane	--	Isabella	--	Ramelton	Donegal	1849	Superior	Derry
Steel	Joseph	--	Elizabeth	--	--	--	1811	Harmony	Derry
			Sally	--					
Stephenson	Alexander	--			N'tnstewart	Tyrone	1850	Lumley	Derry
Stephenson	Charles	29			Fintragh	Donegal	1804	Jefferson	Bally-shannon
Stephenson	John	27			Fintragh	Donegal	1804	Jefferson	Bally-shannon
Stephenson	Margaret	22			Fintragh	Donegal	1804	Jefferson	Bally-shannon
Stephenson	William	20			Fintragh	Donegal	1804	Jefferson	Bally-shannon
Stevenson	James	--			Kilmacrenan	Donegal	1849	Garland	Derry
Stevenson	Janet	--	Jane	--	Raphoe	Donegal	1849	Garland	Derry
			Martha	12					
Stevenson	Thomas	21			Dunaghy	Antrim	1804	Commerce	--
Stewart	Alexander	20			Kereight	Wexford	1803	Strafford	Derry
Stewart	Alexander	21			Tullish	Down	1803	George	Belfast
Stewart	Andrew	--			Fanad	Donegal	1850	Envoy	Derry
Stewart	Anne	18			Belfast	Antrim	1804	Commerce	--

ULSTER EMIGRANTS TO PHILADELPHIA

Last Name	First Name	Age	Family	Age	Address	County	Date	Ship	Port
Stewart	Daniel	--	Isabella	--	Letterkenny	Donegal	1848	MaryCampbell	Derry
			William	--					
Stewart	David	--	Eleanor	--	Castlederg	Tyrone	1848	HannahKerr	Derry
			Eliza	--					
			Nancy	--					
			John	12					
Stewart	James	10			Castlederg	Tyrone	1848	HannahKerr	Derry
Stewart	James	19			Crevolea	Derry	1833-34 --		Derry
Stewart	James	25			Dungiven	Derry	1803	Penna.	Derry
Stewart	John	--	Eliza	--	Lifford	(*)	1850	Envoy	Derry
			MarthaJane	--					
			Robert	--					
			Elizabeth	14					
			Margaret	12					
			John	9					
Stewart	John	--	Robert	--	Letterkenny	Donegal	1848	MaryCampbell	Derry
			Jane	--					
			MaryAnne	--					
			George	--					
Stewart	John	18			Drumore	Derry	1833-34--		Derry
Stewart	John	40	Jane	40	Ballymore	Derry	1833-34--		Derry
			Wiliam	16					
			John	14					
			Robert	12					
			Hugh	8					
			Eliz.	6					
			Mary Ann						
Stewart	Manes	--			Eskaheen	Donegal	1850	Superior	Derry
Stewart	Margaret	--			Letterkenny	Donegal	1847	Hartford	Derry
Stewart	Margaret	30			Clintagh	Derry	1833-34 --		Derry
Stewart	Mary	--			Letterkenny	Donegal	1850	Superior	Derry
Stewart	Rebecca	--			Millford	Donegal	1848	MaryCampbell	Derry
Stewart	William	25			Coleraine	Derry	1803	Brutus	Derry

ULSTER EMIGRANTS TO PHILADELPHIA

Last Name	First Name	Age	Family	Age	Address	County	Date	Ship	Port
Stewart	William	50	Margaret	38	--	--	1803	Active	Newry
			Ann	24					
			Agnes	20					
			Susannah	18					
Stinson	John	20			Glenconway	Derry	1833-34--		Derry
Stirling	Henry	--	Elizabeth	--	Coleraine	Derry	1847	Hartford	Derry
			James	--					
			Esther	--					
			Henry	--					
			Robert	--					
			Wilson	11					
			Eliza	9					
Stirling	Thomas	--	Martha	--	--	--	1811	Harmony	Derry
Strachan	James	20			Connor	Antrim	1803	George	Belfast
Summerville	Mary Ann	--			Strabane	Tyrone	1847	MaryStewart	Derry
Swan	James	--	Elizabeth	--	Cross	(*)	1850	superior	Derry
			George	--					
			Elizabeth	10					
			Jane	6					
			James	2					
Swan	Samuel	--	Isabella	--	Cross	(*)	1850	Superior	Derry
			Paul	--					
			Mary	--					
			Martha	--					
			Thomas	12					
Swan	Thomas	--	Matilda	--	Limavady	Derry	1847	Allegheny	Derry
			John	3					
			Samuel	1					
Sweeney	Phil	--			Rosnakill	Donegal	1850	Superior	Derry
Sweeny	Bridget	--			Ramelton	Donegal	1847	Barbara	Derry
Sweeny	Charles	--			Crossroads	Donegal	1847	Montpellier	Derry
Sweeny	Edward	--			Birdstown	Donegal	1849	Superior	Derry

(*) See Endnotes

ULSTER EMIGRANTS TO PHILADELPHIA

Last Name	First Name	Age	Family	Age	Address	County	Date	Ship	Port
Sweeny	John	--	Cath'ne	Ann	Ramelton	Donegal	1847	Superior	Derry
Sweeny	Mary	--			Coleraine	Derry	1849	Superior	Derry
Sweeny	Michael	--	Catherine	--	Dunfanaghy	Derry	1849	Envoy	Derry
			Patrick	--					
			Michael	--					
			John	8					
			Charles	5					
			James	1					
Sweeny	Neal	--			Carrygalt	Donegal	1847	Hartford	Derry
Sweeny	Patrick	--	Catherine	--	Buncrana	Donegal	1847	Allegheny	Derry
Syms	James	45	Mary	40	Killartie	Donegal	1804	Catherine	Bally-shannon
			Samuel	6					
			Elizabeth	4					
Syms	John	30	Catherine	21	Glen	Donegal	1804	Catherine	Bally-shannon
Tagart	Joseph	--			--	--	1811	Mary	Derry
Taggart	Alice	--			Ballybofey	Donegal	1848	HannahKerr	Derry
Tait	James	36			Armagh	Armagh	1803	Mohawk	Derry
Taylor	Fanny	--			L'Derry	Derry	1847	Barbara	Derry
Taylor	James	--			Coleraine	Derry	1847	MaryStewart	Derry
Taylor	James	--			Ramelton	Donegal	1850	Envoy	Derry
Taylor	James	--	Martha	--	Castlederg	Tyrone	1847	Superior	Derry
			James	--					
			Stephen	--					
			Thomas	--					
Taylor	William	--	Nancy	--	Maghera	Donegal	1849	Superior	Derry
			Jane	8					
			Isaac	5					
			Betty	3					
			William	3m					
			David	--					
Tease	John	--			Millford	Donegal	1848	MaryCampbell	Derry
Tease	Samuel	--	Margaret	--	Millford	Donegal	1848	MaryCampbell	Derry

ULSTER EMIGRANTS TO PHILADELPHIA

Last Name	First Name	Age	Family	Age	Address	County	Date	Ship	Port
Tedley	Henry	--			Muff	Derry	1847	Allegheny	Derry
Teel	Margaret	26			Clanely	Tyrone	1803	Penna.	Derry
Tehan	Patrick	--	Ann	--	Ballyshannon	Donegal	1849	Envoy	Derry
			Bessy	2					
Temple	Ann	--	Isabella	--	Fintona	Tyrone	1847	Hartford	Derry
			James	--					
			Mary Ann	11					
			Hamilton	7					
			John	4					
			Andrew	2					
Templeton	Elizabeth	--			Buncrana	Donegal	1849	Envoy	Derry
Thompson	Alexander	--			Churchill	Donegal	1849	Superior	Derry
Thompson	Alexander	30			Letterkenny	Donegal	1803	Brutus	Derry
Thompson	Ann	--			Clondermott	Derry	1849	Superior	Derry
Thompson	Ann	--			Coleraine	Derry	1849	Envoy	Derry
Thompson	Edward	34	Edward	8	Lurgan	(*)	1804	Jefferson	Bally-shannon
Thompson	Fanny Ann	--			Clondermot	Derry	1847	Venice	Derry
Thompson	Hugh	36			Kilmore	Down	1804	Commerce	--
Thompson	James	--			--	--	1811	Mary	Derry
Thompson	James	25			Donegal	Donegal	1803	Brutus	Derry
Thompson	John	--	Thomas	--	Raphoe	Donegal	1849	Envoy	Derry
Thompson	John	24			Lurgan	(*)	1804	Jefferson	Bally-shannon
Thompson	John	28			Ballymoney	Antrim	1803	George	Belfast
Thompson	John	35			Ardmalin	Donegal	1803	Mohawk	Derry
Thompson	Mary	--			Strabane	Tyrone	1848	HannahKerr	Derry
Thompson	Mary	22			Lurgan	(*)	1804	Jefferson	Bally-shannon
Thompson	Robert	--			--	--	1811	Harmony	Derry
Thompson	Sally	30			Terrydremont	Derry	1833-34	--	Derry
Thompson	Samuel	28	Anna	30	Dungannon	Tyrone	1803	Mohawk	Derry

(*) See Endnotes

88

ULSTER EMIGRANTS TO PHILADELPHIA

Last Name	First Name	Age	Family	Age	Address	County	Date	Ship	Port
(Cont'd.)			Andrew	25					
			Sarah	22					
			James	6					
Thompson	Thomas	23			Castlefin	Donegal	1804	Brothers	Derry
Thorne	John	--			--	--	1811	Mary	Derry
Tiffany	Daniel	24			Rossinver	Leitrim	1804	Jefferson	Bally-shannon
Tiffords	George	28			--	Down	1803	Patty	Newry
Timoly	Mathew	28			Ballymenagh	Down	1803	George	Belfast
Todd	James	20			Ballindrait	Donegal	1803	Penna.	Derry
Tolan	Brien	--			Fanad	Donegal	1849	Superior	Derry
Toland	Daniel	--			Clonmany	Donegal	1847	Hartford	Derry
Toland	Daniel	--			L'Derry	Derry	1849	Superior	Derry
Tonar	Jane	--	Margaret	--	Lisglass	Derry	1849	Superior	Derry
			SarahJane	9					
Toner	Mary	--			Malin	Donegal	1849	Superior	Derry
Toole	Marcus	39	Jane	28	Belfast	Antrim	1803	George	Belfast
Torrers	Samuel	--	Ruth	--	--	--	1811	Fame	Derry
			Samuel	--					
			Ann	--					
Towel	James	22			--	--	1803	Edward	Belfast
Tracy	Bernard	--			Claudy	Derry	1850	Superior	Derry
Treaner	Margaret	--			Draperstown	Derry	1850	Superior	Derry
Tully	Mary	--			Ballybofey	Donegal	1848	HannahKerr	Derry
Turbett	Edward	--			Beragh	Tyrone	1849	Superior	Derry
Turbett	Samuel	--			Portstewart	Derry	1850	Superior	Derry
Turner	Mary	--	Samuel	3	Ramelton	Donegal	1847	Venice	Derry
			James	1					
Vance	Charles	--			Buncrana	Donegal	1848	HannahKerr	Derry
Vance	Elizabeth	--			Ballybofey	Donegal	1848	HannahKerr	Derry
Vance	James	--			Moville	Donegal	1847	Hartford	Derry
Wade	Isaac	--			Lisdillon	Derry	1848	HannahKerr	Derry
Waker	James	40			--	--	1804	Maria	Derry

ULSTER EMIGRANTS TO PHILADELPHIA

Last Name	First Name	Age	Family	Age	Address	County	Date	Ship	Port
Walker	Ann	24			--	--	1804	Maria	Derry
Walker	David	--			Omagh	Tyrone	1847	Hartford	Derry
Walker	George	20			Stewartstown	Tyrone	1803	Mohawk	Derry
Walker	James	32	Ann	30	Enniskillen	Fermanagh	1803	Mohawk	Derry
Walker	Joseph	--			Fahan	Donegal	1847	Hartford	Derry
Walker	Ralph	36	Anne	32	Enniskillen	Fermanagh	1803	Mohawk	Derry
Walker	William	30	MaryAnn	20	Coagh	Tyrone	1803	Strafford	Derry
			Elizabeth	18					
Wallace	James	--			L'Derry	Derry	1850	Superior	Derry
Wallace	Samuel	--			--	--	1811	Mary	Derry
Wallace	Sarah	--			L'Derry	Derry	1850	Superior	Derry
Walsh	Robert	22			Downpatrick	Down	1803	George	Belfast
Ward	James	--	Mary	--	Castlegrove	Galway	1850	Lumley	Derry
Ward	Margaret	--	Catherine	--	Ramelton	Donegal	1847	Venice	Derry
			Phillip	--					
			James	--					
			Richard	--					
			William	--					
Wark	David	--			Ballybofey	Donegal	1848	HannahKerr	Derry
Wark	Elizabeth	--	Ellen	--	Redcastle	Queens	1849	Garland	Derry
			Eliza	--					
			Margaret	11					
Wark	Isaac	20			Ballywoodstock	Derry	1834	--	Derry
Wason	Archer	--	Jane	--	--	--	1811	Mary	Derry
Waters	Ann	--			Claudy	Derry	1849	Garland	Derry
Waters	Charles	--	Mary	--	Rathmullan	Donegal	1849	Envoy	Derry
			Michael	6m					
Waters	Hugh	--			Gartica	Derry	1850	Superior	Derry
Waters	John	--			Muff	Derry	1849	Superior	Derry
Watley	Rebecca	--			Coleraine	Derry	1848	MaryCampbell	Derry
Watson	Rebecca	--			Strabane	Tyrone	1847	Alleghany	Derry
Watt	Arthur	--	PeggyAnn	--	Coleraine	Derry	1847	Hartford	Derry
			Betty Ann	2					

ULSTER EMIGRANTS TO PHILADELPHIA

Last Name	First Name	Age	Family	Age	Address	County	Date	Ship	Port
Watt	James	--			N'tncunningham	Donegal	1847	Hershell	Derry
Watt	Robert	--	William	--	Drumskellan	Donegal	1849	Garland	Derry
Waugh	Sarah	--	Elizabeth	--	Ballybofey	Donegal	1848	HannahKerr	Derry
Weir	Mary	--			Creeslough	Donegal	1847	MaryStewart	Derry
Westley	John	24			Coleraine	Derry	1833	--	Derry
Westley	John	24			Tullans	Derry	1833-34	--	Derry
White	Mary Jane	--			Stranorlar	Donegal	1850	Envoy	Derry
White	Michael	--	Pat	--	Carlow	Carlow	1850	Superior	Derry
			Biddy	--					
White	William	18			Ballyshannon	Donegal	1803	Penna.	Derry
Wiley	Jane	--			St.Johnston	Donegal	1849	Envoy	Derry
Wiley	Samuel	--	Sarah	--	L'Derry	Derry	1847	Venice	Derry
Wilkins	William	--			Creeslough	Donegal	1850	Envoy	Derry
Wilkinson	John	23			N'tnstewart	Tyrone	1803	Brutus	Derry
Wilkinson	Nancy	--			Buncrana	Donegal	1850	Envoy	Derry
Williams	Elizabeth	--			Ramelton	Donegal	1850	Lumley	Derry
Williams	George	--			--	--	1811	Mary	Derry
Williams	Henry	28			--	Armagh	1803	Patty	Newry
Williams	Patrick	--	Nancy	--	Ramelton	Donegal	1847	Hershell	Derry
Williams	William	--			--	--	1811	Mary	Derry
Willoughan	Mary	--			Castleder	Tyrone	1848	MaryCampbell	Derry
Wilson	Anne	--	Martha	10	Letterkenny	Donegal	1847	MaryStewart	Derry
Wilson	Charles	25			Pottagh	Derry	1834	--	Derry
Wilson	Edward	18			--	--	1803	Edward	Belfast
Wilson	Eleanor	36			Limavady	Derry	1803	Penna.	Derry
Wilson	Henry	24			Belfast	Antrim	1803	George	Belfast
Wilson	Isabella	--			Castleder	Tyrone	1848	HannahKerr	Derry
Wilson	James	20			N'tnconningham	Donegal	1803	Brutus	Derry
Wilson	John	--			--	--	1811	Fame	Derry
Wilson	John	--			Fintona	Tyrone	1848	HannahKerr	Derry
Wilson	John	19			N'tnconningham	Donegal	1803	Brutus	Derry
Wilson	John	20			Clagan	Derry	1833-34	--	Derry
Wilson	John	22			--	--	1803	Strafford	Derry

ULSTER EMIGRANTS TO PHILADELPHIA

Last Name	First Name	Age	Family	Age	Address	County	Date	Ship	Port
Wilson	John	56	Samuel	45	Muff	Derry	1803	Penna.	Derry
			James	20					
Wilson	Joseph	22			Belfast	Antrim	1803	George	Belfast
Wilson	Nancy	--	John	--	Garvagh	Derry	1847	Barbara	Derry
			MaryAnn	--					
			Ellen	13					
			Christianna	8					
			Samuel	5					
			Matilda	3					
Wilson	Thomas	25	Nancy	26	St.Johnston	Donegal	1803	Penna.	Derry
Wilson	William	--			Killygordon	(*)	1847	Barbara	Derry
Wisely	John	--			Downhill	Derry	1847	Hartford	Derry
Wishart	James	51			Dungannon	Tyrone	1804	Brothers	Derry
Wishart	Margaret	21			Pettigoe	(*)	1804	Brothers	Derry
Wishat	Robert	--	Sarah	--	--	--	1811	Mary	Derry
			Mary	--					
			Ruth	--					
			Sarah	--					
Wisley	Martin	18	Margaret	45	Bolea	Derry	1833-34	--	Derry
Witherow	James	--	Easter	--	Elagh	Tyrone	1849	Superior	Derry
			Emelia	10					
			Rebecca	7					
			William	5					
			Isabella	3					
Witherow	Thomas	--			Limavady	Derry	1848	HannahKerr	Derry
Wood	Alexander	26	Mary	20	Lisnaskea	Fermanagh	1803	Mohawk	Derry
Woods	Adam	--			--	--	1811	Mary	Derry
Woods	James	--			--	--	1811	Mary	Derry
Wright	James	24			Boghill	Derry	1833-34	--	Derry
Young	James	--	Hugh	--	Castlederg	Tyrone	1848	MaryCampbell	Derry
Young	John	--	Mary	--	--	--	1811	Harmony	Derry
Young	Martha	--			Ballybofey	Donegal	1848	HannahKerr	Derry

(*) See Endnotes

ULSTER EMIGRANTS TO PHILADELPHIA

Last Name	First Name	Age	Family	Age	Address	County	Date	Ship	Port
Young	Mary Ann	--			Waterside	Derry	1850	Superior	Derry
Young	Noble	22	James	21	Pethgow	Fermanagh	1804	Brothers	Derry
			Sarah	50					
Young	William	--			Castlederg	Tyrone	1847	Superior	Derry
Young	William	25			Shanloughead	Derry	1834	--	Derry

TOWN AND COUNTY LISTINGS IN INDEX

TOWN AND COUNTY LISTINGS IN INDEX

TOWN AND COUNTY LISTINGS IN INDEX

TOWN AND COUNTY LISTINGS IN INDEX

Address	County	Address	County
Glebe	Derry	Killygordon	(*)
Glen	Donegal	Kilmacrenan	Donegal
Glenalla	Donegal	Kilmore	Down
Glenconway	Derry	Knackan	Derry
Glenfin	Roscommon	Knocknogher	Derry
Glengivney	?	Laghy	Donegal
Glenmore	(*)	Lands Agivey	Derry
Glenties	Donegal	Largy	Derry
Glentogher	Donegal	Largyreagh	Derry
Glenwinny	Fermanagh	Learmount	Derry
Gobnascale	Donegal	Leck	(*)
Gortahork	Donegal	Letter	Donegal
Gorticross	Derry	Letterkenny	Donegal
Gortin	(*)	Lifford	(*)
Gortnarne	Derry	Limavady	Derry
Gowshill	Tyrone	Lisboy	Derry
Grange	Down	Lisdillon	Derry
Grorty?	?	Lisglass	Derry
Hornhead	Donegal	Lislane	Derry
Innishannon	Donegal	Lisnacloon	Tyrone
Keady	Armagh	Lisnamuck	Derry
Kereight	Wexford	Lisnaskea	Fermanagh
Kesh	Fermanagh	Lissan	Tyrone
Killarhel	Donegal	Lochris	Donegal
Killartie	Donegal	Londonderry	Derry
Killashandra	Cavan	Loughill	Antrim
Killea	Derry	Loughinisland	Down
Killeaton	Antrim	Loughlin	Donegal
Killeter	Tyrone	Lowtherstown	Fermanagh
Killinchy	Down	Lurgan	(*)
Killoyle	Derry	Maghera	Donegal
Killybegs	Donegal	Magherafelt	Derry

TOWN AND COUNTY LISTINGS IN INDEX

Address	County	Address	County
Magheragill	Down	Racecourse	Galway
Magheramore	Derry	Raferty	Donegal
Magilligan	Derry	Ragargam?	?
Malin	Donegal	Ramelton	Donegal
Meenhallu	Donegal	Raphoe	Donegal
Milford	Mayo	Rathmullan	Donegal
Millford	Donegal	Redcastle	Queens
M'nrcunningham	Donegal	Rosnakill	Donegal
Moboy	(*)	Rosses	Donegal
Monargan	Donegal	Rossgole	Fermanagh
Moneycarris	Derry	Rossinver	Leitrim
Moneymore	(*)	Sea Patrick	Down
Monksfield	Galway	Seaford	Down
Moville	Donegal	Shanloughead	Derry
Muff	Derry	Sistrakeel	Derry
Mullaghmore	Derry	Six Mile Cross	Tyrone
Newbuildings	(*)	St.Johnston	Donegal
Newton	Donegal	St.Johnstown	Donegal
N'tnconningham	Donegal	Stewartstown	Tyrone
N'tncunningham	Donegal	Strabane	Tyrone
N'tnstewart	Tyrone	Straid	(*)
Omagh	Tyrone	Stranorlar	Donegal
Oughtymore	Derry	Taghboyne	Westmeath
Pethgow	Fermanagh	Tamlaght Finlagan	Derry
Pettigoe	(*)	Tamney	Donegal
Plumbridge	Derry	Tarnakelly	Derry
Portglenone	Antrim	Taughblane	Down
Portlough	Donegal	Templemoyle	(*)
Portrush	Antrim	Tempo	Fermanagh
Portstewart	Derry	Termaquin	Derry
Pottagh	Derry	Termon	Donegal
Prehen	Derry	Terrydoo	Derry

TOWN AND COUNTY LISTINGS IN INDEX

ENDNOTES

Addresses Found in More Than One County

Aughnacloy	Tyrone, Armagh, Down, Monahan, Sligo.
Ballygawley	Derry, Donegal, Tyrone.
Balteagh	Armagh, Derry.
Carrakeel	Derry, Donegal.
Clogher	Antrim, Down, Donegal, Fermanagh, Galway.
Clooney	Antrim, Donegal, Derry.
Craigs	Antrim, Donegal, Tyrone.
Coss	Antirm, Donegal, Down, Fermanagh, Galway, Mayo, Sligo.
Dooey	Antrim, Derry, Dondgal, Down.
Dromore	Antrim, Derry, Donegal, Down, Fermanagh, Mayo, Roscommon, Sligo, Tyrone.
Farmhill	Galway, Mayo..
Fountainhill	Galway, Mayo
Gallagh	Antrim, Fermanagh, Monaghan, Roscommon, Tyrone.
Glenmore	Galway, Monaghan, Roscommon.
Gortin	Antrim, Derry, Donegal, Tyrone.
Killygordon	Donegal, Tyrone.
Leck	Antrim, Cavan, Derry, Monaghan, Tyrone.
Lifford	Donegal, Tyrone.
Lurgan	Armagh, Cavan, Donegal Fermanagh, Galway, Mayo, Roscommon.
Moboy	Antrim, Tyrone.
Moneymore	Derry, Donegal, Mayo, Roscommon.

ENDNOTES

Addresses Found in More Than One County

Newbuildings	Antrim, Derry, Tyrone.
Pettigoe	Donegal, Fermanagh.
Straid	Antrim, Derry, Donegal, Galway.
Templemoyle	Derry, Donegal, Galway.

www.ingramcontent.com/pod-product-compliance
Lightning Source LLC
Chambersburg PA
CBHW071055280326
41928CB00050B/2516